Thrive!® - Quick Guide To A Thriving Future

by

Gary "Chris" Christopherson
Founder, *Thrive!*® - Building a Thriving Future
Founder, Health*e*People® - Building a Healthy and Thriving Future

Nelson, WI   University Park, MD

DEDICATION

People who help build, achieve and sustain

a surviving and thriving future for all forever.

Irene and Lynn Christopherson, nurturing and inspiring parents.

Dr. Patricia Haeuser, friend and supporter.

Thrive!

About The Author

Gary (Chris) Christopherson continues to work nationally and locally on improving health, reducing vulnerability and building a better future. Currently at The Thrive! Center he founded, he develops strategy, management and policy for creating, managing and sustaining large positive change and building a better and thriving future for all forever. www.ThrivingFuture.org He wrote the nonfiction book **Thrive! - Building a Thriving Future** available via www.Amazon.com or www.ThrivingFuture.org.

Thrive! draws on his 30+ years experience creating, managing and sustaining large positive change at national and local levels in public and private sectors. He founded HealthePeople (building a healthy and thriving future; www.HealthePeople.com), *via*Future (creating large positive change) and **Vulnerable** (minimizing vulnerability). He served as a senior leader, manager and policymaker responsible for multi-billion dollar policy, programs and budgets and thousands of employees. His public service includes: Principal Deputy Assistant Secretary and Acting Assistant Secretary of Defense for Health Affairs and Senior Advisor, Department of Defense; Associate Director, Presidential Personnel, Executive Office of the President, White House; Senior Fellow, National Academy of Public Administration; Senior Advisor to Chief Operating Officer and Deputy Director for the Quality Improvement Group, Centers for Medicare and Medicaid Services, DHHS; Senior Advisor to Under Secretary, Veterans Health Administration, VA; Senior Fellow and Scholar-In-Residence, Institute of Medicine, National Academy of Sciences; Chief Information Officer, Veterans Health Administration, VA; Director of Health Legislation, House Select Committee on Aging, U.S. House of Representatives; and Deputy Director, Municipal Health Services Program (funded by The Robert Wood Johnson Foundation and based at John Hopkins Medical Institutions).

He is a sculptor of abstract art, focusing on mobile and stabile sculptures and creating over 150 sculptures. GChris Sculpture at www.GChris.com. He wrote several science fiction books, including **black box** and the illustrated children's book **Angel, Thriving Creator of Artful Things**. All are available via www.Amazon.com or www.GChris.com.

He received his bachelor's in political science and his master's in urban and regional planning from the University of Wisconsin – Madison, and did doctoral work in health policy and management at John Hopkins University School of Public Health.

Table of Contents

Thrive!® - Quick Guide To A Thriving Future i

About The Author iv

Table of Contents v

Brief Summary vi

Summary vii

Chapter 1: How to use this Quick Guide. 1

Chapter 2: What a thriving future will be. 5

Chapter 3: Why care about a thriving future. 9

Chapter 4: How you and your family and friends can thrive. 15

Chapter 5: How you and your community can thrive 27

Chapter 6: How you and your country can thrive 41

Chapter 7: How our world can thrive. 55

Chapter 8: Thrive! System© (TS). Achieve thriving people and communities with highest levels of thriving for all everywhere. 69

Chapter 9: How the *Thrive!* Endeavor, you and all of us together, builds a thriving future. 93

Example and Worksheets 101

Thrive!

Brief Summary

This **<u>Quick Guide To A Thriving Future</u>** is provided to help you and your family and friends, community, country and world survive and thrive.[1] It shows how to build a thriving future using *Thrive!* **Strategy and Action Plans**. The "Quick Guide" quickly takes you through the basics of building a thriving future.[2]

For our selves, our future generations and the Earth on which we depend, you and we must, can and will achieve a surviving and thriving future for all forever. This future is *Thrive!* and is a bold vision and mission. This Guide describes what your life and your world will be in a thriving future where all survive and thrive forever, to the maximum extent possible. It lays out why you and we must care about a surviving and thriving future for you, your friends and family, your community, your country and our world. You and we all want and need that future because of our endangered future and our human need to survive and desire to thrive. The Guide shows you and all of us how to build, achieve and sustain a surviving and thriving future for you and your friends and family, your community, your country and our world. And yes, we can as we are now the most able in human history. To help achieve this better future, the *Thrive!* **Next Generation Toolkit** provides next generation strategy and tools.   Finally, this guide shows how the *Thrive!* **Endeavor**, you and all of us together, builds, achieves and sustains <u>a thriving future</u> <u>for all</u> <u>forever</u>.

---

[1] This **<u>Quick Guide</u>** and the more comprehensive **People's Guide**, including larger, fillable worksheets, can be downloaded free from www.ThrivingFuture.org

[2] You might also want to use *Thrive!* **- Building a Thriving Future** - a manual providing greater depth on strategy and tools and which is available via www.Amazon.com or as free download from www.ThrivingFuture.org.

Summary

This **<u>Quick Guide To A Thriving Future</u>** shows how to build a thriving future using *Thrive!* **Strategy and Action Plans**.[3] The "Quick Guide" quickly takes you through the basics of building a thriving future.[4]

How to use this Guide. (Chapter 1) This Guide helps you and your family and friends, community, country and world survive and thrive. For our selves, our future generations and our Earth on which we depend, you and all of us must, can and will achieve a surviving and thriving future. This Guide describes what your life and world will be in a thriving future where all survive and thrive forever, to the maximum extent possible. It lays out why you and all of us must care about a surviving and thriving future. All of us want and need that future because of our endangered future and our human need to survive and desire to thrive. This Guide shows you how to build, achieve and sustain a surviving and thriving future for you and your friends and family, community, country and world. We can as we are now the most able in human history. To help achieve this better future, the *Thrive!* **Next Generation Toolkit** provides next generation strategy and tools. Finally, this guide shows how the *Thrive!* **Endeavor**, you and all of us together, builds, achieves and sustains <u>a thriving future</u> <u>for all</u> <u>forever</u>.

What a thriving future will be. (Chapter 2) This Guide describes what your life and our world will be in a thriving future where all survive and thrive forever, to the maximum extent possible. This future is *Thrive!* and is a bold vision and mission. It is different and better than anything tried or achieved in human history. It is a <u>thriving</u> future, not just getting by or achieving a surviving future. It is a thriving future for <u>all people and all</u> <u>future generations</u>, a "50+ generation" strategy. Not just for some people or just for the current or next generation. It is a thriving future <u>forever</u>, a 1000+ year strategy. Not just for today or just 100 years. It is also for <u>the</u> <u>Earth on which we live and depend</u>, not just for people.

Why you and all of us must care about a thriving future. (Chapter 3) This Guides lays out why you and all of us must care about a surviving and <u>thriving future for you</u>, your friends and family, your community, your

---

[3] This **<u>Quick Guide</u>** and the more comprehensive **People's Guide**, including larger, fillable worksheets, can be downloaded free from <u>www.ThrivingFuture.org</u>

[4] You might also want to use ***Thrive! - <u>Building a Thriving Future</u>*** - a manual providing greater depth on strategy sund tools and which is available via <u>www.Amazon.com</u> or as free download from <u>www.ThrivingFuture.org</u>.

country and our world. You and all of us want and need that future because of our endangered future and our human need to survive and desire to thrive. What drives us is that a person and a people need to survive and desire to thrive in the current world and a sustainable future world. Further, because it is people who broke much of the world and endangered its future, it is people who must fix what is broken and build a survivable and thriving future for all forever.

How you and all of us can build a surviving and thriving future for you, all of us and those we care about. (Guide Chapters 4 through 7) Can we? Keep in mind that we are more able than any time in human history. We can build a thriving future by effectively and collaboratively using all available knowledge and tools, including next generation *Thrive!* strategy and tools. Next generation *Thrive!* is different and better than anything in human history. It is <u>achieving</u> a thriving future at each level. It understands that <u>people's behavior</u>, including yours, makes (or breaks) a thriving future. It helps you and all of us achieve the behavior that in turn achieves a thriving future at each level and for all forever.

How can we do it for you and those you care about? Chapter 4 shows you how to build, achieve and sustain that future for <u>you and your friends and family</u>. Chapter 5 shows you how to build, achieve and sustain that future for <u>you and your community</u>. Chapter 6 shows you how to build, achieve and sustain that future for <u>you and your country</u>. Chapter 7 shows you how to build, achieve and sustain that future for <u>our world</u>. Each chapter includes how to build a *Thrive!* **Strategy and Action Plan**. Chapter 8 shows you **Thrive! Systems**, how to use such a system to build, achieve and sustain a thriving future for <u>you and your community</u>.

How the *Thrive!* Endeavor, you and all of us together, builds a thriving future. (Chapter 9) <u>All of us together</u>, <u>including you</u>, must and can build a thriving future for all forever via the *Thrive!* **Endeavor**. It is only people that can and must fix what is broken and build a survivable and thriving future. It will take all of us. For these reasons, *Thrive!* is and requires a vast, sustained people endeavor building and sustaining a surviving and thriving future for all forever. Creating and sustaining this vast *Thrive!* **Endeavor** and a surviving and thriving future for all forever is the driving purpose of this **Guide**.[5]

---

[5] You might also want to use *Thrive!* **- Building a Thriving Future** - a manual providing greater depth on strategy and tools and which is available via www.Amazon.com or as free download from www.ThrivingFuture.org.

Chapter 1: How to use this <u>Quick Guide</u>.
How to use this **<u>Quick Guide</u>** to help you and your family and friends, community, country and world survive and thrive forever.

This **<u>Quick Guide To A Thriving Future</u>** is provided to help you and your family and friends, community, country and world survive and thrive forever.[6] For our selves, our future generations and the Earth on which we depend, you and we must, can and will achieve a surviving and thriving future for all forever.[7] This future is ***Thrive!***, a bold vision and mission.

In this Guide, the term ***Thrive!*** ® has several meanings:[8]
- ***Thrive!*** is the <u>vision</u> of a thriving and surviving future forever for all (our selves, family and friends, communities, countries and world).
- ***Thrive!*** is the <u>human aspiration</u> to build, achieve and sustain a surviving and thriving future for all forever.
- ***Thrive!*** is the <u>mission</u> to create and sustain large, positive and timely change that builds and achieves a surviving and thriving future for all forever.
- ***Thrive!*** is the <u>call to action and rallying cry</u> to build, achieve and sustain a surviving and thriving future for all forever.

---

[6] This **<u>Quick Guide</u>** and the more comprehensive **<u>People's Guide</u>**, including larger, fillable worksheets, can be downloaded free from <u>www.ThrivingFuture.org</u>
[7] Whenever the term "thriving future" is used, it means "a thriving future for all forever, to the maximum extent possible". For example, while an individual person may not survive (live) and thrive forever, people (human race) may survive and thrive forever, whether on Earth or another inhabitable planet.
[8] The ***Thrive!*** trademark is registered to Gary Christopherson.

Thrive!

- ***Thrive!*** is the vast ***<u>Thrive!</u> Endeavor*** by all of us to build, achieve and sustain a surviving and thriving future for all forever.

This Guide describes what your life and your world will be in a thriving future where all survive and thrive forever, to the maximum extent possible. It lays out why you and we must care about a surviving and thriving future for you, your friends and family, your community, your country and our world. You and all of us want and need that future because of our endangered future and our human need to survive and desire to thrive. This Guide shows you how to build, achieve and sustain a surviving and thriving future for you, your friends and family, your community, your country and our world. And yes, we can as we are now the most able in human history. To help, ***Thrive!*** provides next generation strategy and tools. Finally, this guide shows how the ***Thrive!*** **Endeavor**, you and all of us together, builds, achieves and sustains <u>a surviving and thriving future</u> <u>for all</u> <u>forever</u>.

More specifically, this Guide describes what your life and your world will be in a thriving future where all survive and thrive forever, to the maximum extent possible. ***Thrive!*** is different and arguably better than anything tried or achieved in human history. It is a <u>thriving</u> future. Not just getting by or achieving a surviving future. A surviving future is necessary but not sufficient. It is a thriving future for <u>all people and all future generations</u>, a "50+ generation" strategy. Not just for some people or just for the current and next generation. It is a thriving future <u>forever</u>, a 1000+ year strategy. Not just for today or just 100 years. It is also for <u>Earth on which we live and depend</u>, not just for people.

So, the first question to ask yourself is whether or not this surviving and thriving future is the future you want? Regardless of how you answer for yourself, then follow other questions. Is this the future your family and friends want? Your community wants? Your country wants? Our world wants? The answer for each of these may be yes, no or not sure.

If you are not sure or do not want this surviving and thriving future, you should read just a bit further. To convince you, this Guide lays out why you and all of us must care about a surviving and thriving future for you, your friends and family, your community, your country and our world. First, you and all of us want and need that future because our future is endangered if we continue our current path. Second, you and all of us want and need that future because we as humans need to survive and strongly desire to thrive in the current world and a sustainable future world. Third, we have an obligation. Because it is people who broke much of the world and endangered its future, it is people who must fix what is broken and build a survivable and thriving future.

But, if you do not want a surviving and thriving future, this Guide has failed in its mission and is probably not for you. Hopefully, you might change your mind in the future.

If you want this future or if you are not sure, you are going to ask if you and we <u>can</u> build, achieve and sustain a surviving and thriving future. You are going to ask <u>how</u>. Chapters 4 through 7 lay out why you and all of us can and how to do it.

You and all of us <u>can</u> because we are more capable than any time in human history. We can build a thriving future by effectively and collaboratively using all available knowledge and tools, including next generation *Thrive!* strategy and tools. Next generation *Thrive!* is different and better than anything in human history. It is <u>achieving</u> a thriving future at each level. It understands that <u>people's behavior</u>, including yours, makes (or breaks) a thriving future. Its knowledge and tools help people, including you, achieve the behavior that in turn achieves a thriving future at each level (family and friends, community, country, world).

<u>How</u> to build and achieve a thriving future for any or all of those you and we care about is laid out as follows.[9]

---

[9] In order to make each "how-to" chapter self-sufficient, there is some necessary repetition. The intent is that each chapter stands on its own depending on who and

- Chapter 4 shows you how to build, achieve and sustain that future for <u>you and your friends and family</u>.
- Chapter 5 shows you how to build, achieve and sustain that future for <u>you and your community</u>.
- Chapter 6 shows you how to build, achieve and sustain that future for <u>you and your country</u>.
- Most ambitiously, Chapter 7 shows you how to build, achieve and sustain that future for <u>our world</u>.
- Chapter 8 shows you **Thrive! Systems**, how to use such a system to build, achieve and sustain a thriving future for <u>you and your community</u>.

This Guide argues <u>why you and all of us should</u> build, achieve and sustain a surviving and thriving future. It argues <u>why we can</u> do it. It walks through <u>how to</u> do it for you and those you and all of us care about. But it will take more than just knowledge and tools and more than just each of us individually. It will take <u>all of us together</u>, <u>including you</u>.

Together, you and all of us must and can build, to the maximum extent possible, a thriving future for all forever via the *Thrive!* **Endeavor**. It is only people that can and must fix what is broken and build a survivable and thriving future. This mission to achieve a thriving future is greater than any in human history and must be sustained for as long as humans exist. To succeed in this mission, it will take all of us working together. For these reasons, *Thrive!* is and requires a vast, sustained endeavor that builds, achieves and sustains a surviving and thriving future for all forever. Creating and sustaining the *Thrive!* **Endeavor** is the driving purpose of this **People's Guide**.[10]

---

what are your priorities (family and friends, community, country, world).

[10] You might also want to use *Thrive! - **Building a Thriving Future*** - a manual providing greater depth on strategy and tools and which is available via www.Amazon.com or as free download from www.ThrivingFuture.org.

Chapter 2: What a thriving future will be.

What your life and your world will be in a thriving future where all survive and thrive forever, to the maximum extent possible.

This Guide describes what your life and your world will be in a thriving future where all survive and thrive forever, to the maximum extent possible. This future is *Thrive!* and is a bold vision and mission.

For you and your family and friends, a thriving future is a better life now and for the near and long term future for all of you and for future generations.

For you and your community, a thriving future is a better life now and for the near and long term future for the whole community and for all of the community's people.

For you and your country, a thriving future is a better life now and for the near and long term future for the whole country and for all of the country's people.

For our world, a thriving future is a better life now and for the near and long term future for the whole world (people and Earth) and for all of the world's people and the Earth itself.

For you and all that you and we care about, it is a much better life and future with less vulnerability, with surviving and with sustained thriving.

Thrive!

When a surviving and thriving future is achieved, you, families and friends, communities, states, countries and the world will be:
- Performing well,
- Well-off (financially),
- Well nourished,
- Well housed,
- Well protected (exposures, crime),
- Well educated,
- Physically and mentally well (people),
- Growing/developing well,
- Living within good habitat,
- Physically well (Earth, plants, animals, environment),
- Not vulnerable,
- Producing personal and public goods,
- Living within a stable, positive climate, and
- Sustained.

When achieved, we will have helped you, families and friends, communities, states, countries and the world move up from:
- Performing poorly or badly,
- Being poor (financially),
- Being poorly nourished,
- Being poorly housed,
- Being poorly protected (exposures, crime),
- Being poorly educated,
- Being physically or mentally ill (people),
- Growing and developing poorly or badly,
- Not doing well "physically" (Earth, plants, animals, environment),
- Living within poor or bad habitat,
- Being excessively vulnerable,
- Living in an unstable, destructive climate, and
- Not being sustained.

Thrive!

When achieved, we will have fulfilled the hope of all, and especially:
- Vulnerable individual people (persons),
- Vulnerable families and friends,
- Vulnerable communities (including neighborhoods, villages, towns, cities, counties, regions),
- Vulnerable states,
- Vulnerable countries, and
- A vulnerable world.

When achieved, we will have:
- Thriving individual people (persons),
- Thriving families and friends,
- Thriving communities (including neighborhoods, villages, towns, cities, counties, states, regions),
- Thriving countries, and
- A thriving world.

Thrive!, a thriving future, is different and arguably better than anything tried or achieved in human history. Not just getting by or achieving a surviving future. A surviving future is necessary but not sufficient. It is a thriving future for <u>all people and all future generations</u>, a "50+ generation" strategy. Not just for some people or just for the current and next generation. It is a thriving future <u>forever</u>, a 1000+ year strategy. Not just for today or just 100 years. It is also for <u>Earth on which we live and depend</u>, not just for people.

Helping achieve this surviving and thriving future is *Thrive!* - a vast human endeavor of you and all of us together striving for a surviving and thriving future. *Thrive!* strives for and envisions a surviving and thriving future, to the maximum extent possible, forever for all (you, family and friends, communities, countries and the world (including the Earth on which it depends).

Thrive!

Chapter 3: Why care about a thriving future.

Why you and we must care about a surviving and thriving future for you. Your friends and family. Your community. Your country. Our world.

This Guides lays out why you and we must care about a surviving and thriving future for you and your friends and family, your community, your country and our world. You and all of us want and need that future because of our endangered future and our human need to survive and desire to thrive. What drives us is that a person and a people <u>need to survive</u> and <u>desire to thrive</u> in the current world and a sustainable future world.

Our needing and desiring a surviving and thriving future is driven by a natural human force - "a person needs to survive and desires to thrive." To truly satisfy this need and desire, we need the following:
1) we, as a person <u>and</u> a people, need to survive and desire to thrive,
2) we depend on <u>other persons</u> (a people) for survival and thriving, especially in the long term,
3) our need and desire applies to both the current <u>and</u> future world,
4) our <u>future</u> survival and thriving depends on there being a <u>future world</u>, and
5) our future world must be <u>sustainable</u> and <u>sustained</u> to fully meet our need and desire.

For these reasons, building, achieving and sustaining a thriving future forever (to the maximum extent possible) for you, your family and friends, your community, your country and our world is <u>the</u> human endeavor and <u>the</u> ideal.

__Thrive!__

This is why you and we care about a thriving future. But let's be a bit more specific.

What future must you and we build, achieve and sustain? You, your family and friends, your community, your country and our world want to and must <u>build, achieve and sustain a surviving and thriving future</u>.

All of us, almost without exception, want to <u>thrive</u>. Thriving means:
- Performing well,
- Being well-off (financially),
- Being well nourished,
- Being well housed,
- Being well protected (exposures, crime),
- Being well educated,
- Being physically and mentally well (people),
- Growing/developing well,
- Living within good habitat,
- Being physically well (Earth, plants, animals, environment),
- Not being vulnerable,
- Producing personal and public goods,
- Living within a stable, positive climate, and
- Being sustained.

This is the best future for you, your family and friends, your community, your country and our world (including the Earth on which we depend).

Thrive!

All of us, almost without exception, want to and must <u>survive</u>.
Surviving means at least:
- Performing at a minimal level,
- Having the minimum levels of resources, food, housing, protection, education, physical and mental health (people), personal growth and development, and habitat,
- Surviving "physically" (Earth, plants, animals, environment),
- Not being excessively vulnerable,
- Producing minimum levels of personal and public goods,
- Being in an humanly survivable climate, and
- Being sustained at a minimal survival level.

This is not the best future but it is far better than not surviving.

What future must we avoid? You, your family and friends, your community, your country and our world want to and must <u>avoid a bad or endangered future</u>. A bad future means:
- Performing poorly or badly,
- Being poor (financially),
- Being poorly nourished,
- Being poorly housed,
- Being poorly protected (exposures, crime),
- Being poorly educated,
- Not being physically or mentally well (people),
- Not growing and developing well,
- Not doing well "physically" (Earth, plants, animals, environment),
- Living within poor or bad habitat,
- Being excessively vulnerable,
- Living in an unstable, destructive climate, and/or
- Not being sustained.

In an endangered future, there is the risk of any or all of these. No one wants to risk this bad future let alone live this bad future.

A bad future also means not fixing what we already know is broken and likely to stay broken.

Thrive!

As we look around us at the people and the world which we care about, much of what is important to us is already broken or is endangered, much of it unnecessarily so. This is probably true for you and your family. This is true for your community, your country and our world.

For example, in the United States, our financial systems' failure did and still could bring down countries' and the world's financial system. Housing bubbles have burst and lifetime savings lost. While some of our housing markets improve, many people cannot buy homes (lack resources, can't get loans, job insecurity) or they own homes they cannot afford or sell. Even with the Affordable Care Act, our health care remains inaccessible, unaffordable and of poor quality for many people. Our education systems leave children behind and fail to educate children to their full potential. Our economic system rewards many people far beyond their contribution, holds many far below their potential contribution, and keeps many in or near poverty. Our environment is under more stress than it can handle in the decades and centuries to come. On energy, our future was bet on non-renewable energy sources and we have yet to turn to conservation and renewable energy at a level commensurate with long term energy needs and supply.

For some countries, the situation is better. For some, it is worse. All countries and the world as a whole are and will continue to be broken to some greater or lesser extent.

But these are only individual broken pieces for us to fix. In the real world, fixing the future means fixing these broken pieces together with fixing related broken pieces, e.g. health with the economy, education with food, energy with the environment, and housing with protection. Fixing these together is more likely to achieve a surviving and thriving future. Fixing all of these together is the most likely to achieve a thriving future.

Because it is people who have broken much of the world and endangered its future, it is people who must care about and must fix what is broken and build a survivable and thriving future. Because it is only people who can change our future, it is people who must build, achieve and sustain a surviving and thriving future.

All of this is why you and we care about a surviving and thriving future.

Chapter 4: How <u>you and your family and friends</u> can thrive.

How to build, achieve and sustain a surviving and thriving future for you and your family and friends.

Why you and your family and friends <u>can</u>.

You and your family and friends <u>can</u> have a surviving and thriving future. To get to that future, keep in mind that each of them is different with a different future already beginning. Each and all of them <u>can</u> do better whether that future appears bad or good. To build a better future, *Thrive!* strategy and tools have been used successfully at the personal level and on larger scales (community, country). They can work for you and the people closest to you. As they have for others, *Thrive!* can help you and your people build, achieve and sustain a surviving and thriving future.

Thrive!
Keep in mind that we are more capable than any time in human history. We can build a thriving future by effectively and collaboratively using all available knowledge and tools, including next generation *Thrive!* strategy and tools. Next generation *Thrive!* is different and better than anything in human history. It is <u>achieving</u> a thriving future at each level. It understands that <u>people's behavior</u>, including yours, makes (or breaks) a thriving future. It helps people, including you, achieve the behavior that in turn achieves a thriving future at each level and for all forever.

Why you and your family and friends <u>must</u>.

You and your family and friends <u>must</u> have a surviving and thriving future. Each and all of your people <u>must</u> do better whether that future appears bad or good. Why? Even those that have a good future are not fully thriving, are not likely to be fully thriving in the future, and are still facing uncertainties about the long term future. You and your people all want and need that future because your and their future is endangered and because of your and their need to survive and desire to thrive. What drives each of them is their need to survive and desire to thrive in the current world and a sustainable future world. Further, because some or all of them have broken some part of their world and endangered its future, you and your people must help fix what is broken and help build a survivable and thriving future.

How to build, achieve, and sustain a surviving and thriving future for you and your family and friends.[11]

To build a surviving and thriving future for you and your family and friends, they should be partners in this endeavor from the beginning and through each step. A collaborative approach where they jointly provide leadership, vision, motivation, strategy and successful execution probably has the greater potential to create <u>and</u> sustain large, positive change and a surviving and thriving future. Key to success is the strong desire to move current vulnerabilities through and beyond surviving to a sustained thriving future. *Thrive!* can be helpful to you and is laid out in the following steps.

---

[11] The following strategy is adapted from the *Thrive!* **Next Generation Toolkit** contained in the Appendix. It is customized to help you and your people build, achieve and sustain a surviving and thriving future. More is available in ***Thrive! - Building a Thriving Future*** - a manual providing greater depth on strategy and tools and is available via www.Amazon.com or free download from www.ThrivingFuture.org.

Step 1.

Step 1. Current state of you and your family and friends. The first major step is to understand the current state of you and your family and friends. This "how-to" works whether it is you alone, you and your immediate family, you and a more extended family, and/or you and your friends. In this chapter, the short-hand term "your people" is used and lets you decide on whom (you alone, you and your immediate family, you and a more extended family, and/or you and your friends) you want to focus your efforts.

a. Who are your people? Let's first go through who are you and your people currently. Who are your people? Use Table 4.1 (end of Quick Guide) to describe each of your people.[12] For each person, have the person independently do a one-paragraph description in her/his own words. If the person can't, do one for the person as best you can. Who is the person with respect to working and living? Financial situation? Eating and drinking? Housing? Protection? Education? Physical and mental health? Personal growth and development? Habitat (living environment)? Producing what? Climate? With this information on individuals and as best you can, do a summary of your people as a whole.

b. How well are they? How well (surviving and thriving) are your people? Use Table 4.2a (end of Quick Guide) to describe how well is each person.[13] How well is each person in terms of performing well? Being well-off (financially)? Being well nourished (food and drink)? Being well housed? Being well protected (exposures, crime)? Being well educated? Being physically and mentally well? Personally growing/developing well? Living within good habitat? Not being vulnerable? Producing personal and public goods? Living within a stable, positive climate? Being sustained? With this information and as best you can, create a summary for your people as a whole. Use Table 4.2b (end of Quick Guide) to describe how well are your people as a whole.[14]

---

[12] Free download of larger, fillable worksheets at www.ThrivingFuture.org
[13] Free download of larger, fillable worksheets at www.ThrivingFuture.org

Answering "yes" to all indicates current surviving and thriving. Though the "yes" answers are good, there is still future work to make sure this continues. "No" answers are bad and mean there is current <u>and</u> future work to be done.

c. What positively or negatively impacts them? What positively or negatively impacts or is likely to impact you and your people's surviving and thriving? Use Table 4.2a (individuals) and 4.2b (summary of your people) to describe all of the following impacts (positive and negative; current and future). What impacts your people's performing well? Being well-off (financially)? Being well nourished (food and drink)? Being well housed? Being well protected (exposures, crime)? Being well educated? Being physically and mentally well? Personally growing/developing well? Living within good habitat? Not being vulnerable? Producing personal and public goods? Living within a stable, positive climate? Being sustained?

Good impacts improve and/or sustain surviving and thriving. If they will continue, you probably can focus on other things. If they may or may not continue, your action is needed to make them continue and/or to develop other things to compensate. Bad impacts prevent or limit surviving and thriving. If they will not continue, you probably can focus on other things. If they may or may not continue, your action is needed to stop them or to avoid or minimize their impact.

Optional. Want more on your people's future and behavior? At this point, you have to go to Step 2 and develop strategy for you and your people. If you want to develop strategy and actions further, you may use the *Thrive!* **Next Generation Toolkit** and optional Sections d-e in the full and Complete Guide versions of the **People's Guide**.

---

[14] Free download of larger, fillable worksheets at www.ThrivingFuture.org

Step 2.

Step 2. Strategy to achieve you and your family and friends' surviving and thriving future. The next major step is to develop the strategy that will help your people build and achieve a surviving and thriving future.

a. Who will your people be in the future? Who will be your future people? If there are any changes to your people that are desired or likely, take them into account. You may want to leave out persons that should not or will not be one of your people. You may want to include future persons that should or will become one of your people (for example, new children, spouse, friend).

For each new person and as you did in Step 1, briefly describe the person to the extent possible. Use Table 4.1 to describe your future people individually and as a whole. What will this person do working and living? Financial situation? Eating and drinking? Housing? Protection? Education? Physical and mental health? Personal growth and development? Quality of habitat (living environment)? Producing what? Climate? If there are likely to be changes on these characteristics with existing members of your people in the future, make these changes as best you can. Also in Table 4.1, do a summary of your people as a whole. This should provide a full picture of your future people (individually and as a whole) as it will be and as desired.

b. How well should your people be in the near and long term future? How well should your people as a whole be in the future? Overall, they should be <u>surviving and thriving</u>. With this as a guide, you and your people choose the surviving and thriving future your people want to build and achieve. The "*Thrive!* strategy" will help you accomplish that.

Use Table 4.3a/b (end of Quick Guide) to describe how well your people should be.[15] Table 4.3a is the simpler version. Table 4.3b is the more detailed and powerful version.

From you and your people's view and to be surviving and thriving, indicate to what extent your people should be performing well. Be well-off (financially). Be well nourished (food and drink). Be well housed. Be well protected (exposures, crime). Be well educated. Be physically and mentally well. Be personally growing/developing well. Be living within good habitat. Not be vulnerable. Be producing personal and public goods. Be living within a stable, positive climate. Be sustained. Again, your people should be surviving and thriving.

c. What has to change externally and internally to achieve your people's thriving future? What has to change externally (outside your people) and internally (within your people) to progress from your people's current status to achieve your desired surviving and thriving status? In Step 1, you identified what positively and negatively impacts or is likely to impact your people. Update those, taking into account any changes to who are your people in the future.

Given those, what has to change externally and internally to achieve a surviving and thriving future? Use Table 4.3a/b to describe all that has to change for the following. To achieve performing well? Being well-off (financially)? Being well nourished (food and drink)? Being well housed? Being well protected (exposures, crime)? Being well educated? Being physically and mentally well? Personally growing/developing well? Living within good habitat? Not being vulnerable? Producing personal and public goods? Living within a stable, positive climate? Being sustained?

Good changes improve and/or sustain surviving and thriving. Bad changes prevent and/or limit surviving and thriving.

d. What actions by your people are needed to achieve their thriving future? What internal actions (by you and your people) and external actions (by others) are needed to bring about the needed external and internal changes (identified in "c") that improve your

---

[15] Free download of larger, fillable worksheets at www.ThrivingFuture.org

people's current status enough to achieve the desired surviving and thriving status? [See Figure 4.1] [16]

External actions by others. There are very important <u>external</u> actions that are needed to support the *Thrive!* strategy. You already identified what has to change externally to achieve your people's surviving and thriving future. What external actions by others will bring about the needed changes?

Use Table 4.3a/b to describe all the external actions to be taken.

Identify external actions by others that support <u>good</u> changes that will help improve and/or sustain surviving and thriving. If good changes are likely to occur, together with others support them. If good changes are not likely to occur, together with others support them and develop other good changes to compensate.

Identify external actions by others that stop <u>bad</u> changes that prevent or limit surviving and thriving. If bad changes are not likely to occur, together with others ensure that they do not. If bad changes are likely to occur, together with others change them, stop them or avoid/reduce their impact.

Internal actions by your people. There are very important <u>internal</u> actions by you and your people that support the *Thrive!* strategy. Individual members and your people as a whole should support your strategy to ensure your people (individually and as a whole) are performing well. Being well-off (financially). Being well nourished (food and drink). Being well housed. Being well protected (exposures, crime). Being well educated. Being physically and mentally well. Personally growing/developing well. Living within good habitat. Not being vulnerable. Producing personal and public goods. Living within a stable, positive climate. Being sustained.

Use Table 4.3a/b to describe all the internal actions to be taken.

---

[16] An action is defined as "who will do what to/with whom, where, when, and with what result."

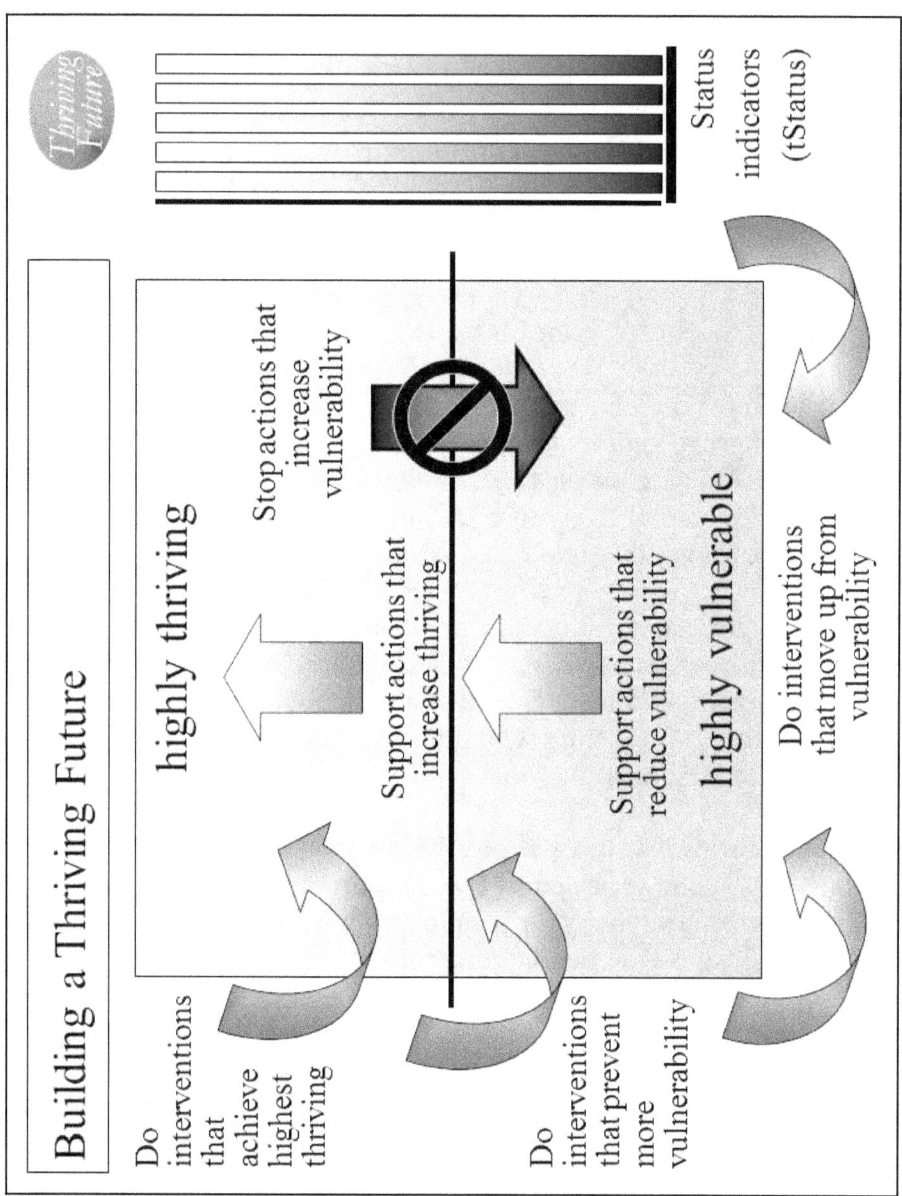

Figure 4.1. Building a Thriving Future.

Identify internal actions by your people that support <u>good</u> changes that will help improve and/or sustain surviving and thriving. If good changes are likely to occur, support them. If good changes are not likely to occur, support them and develop other good changes to compensate. [Use Table 4.3a/b]

Identify internal actions by your people that stop <u>bad</u> changes that prevent or limit surviving and thriving. If bad changes are not likely to occur, ensure that they do not. If bad changes are likely to occur, change them, stop them or avoid/reduce their impact.

e. Overall *Thrive!* strategy and actions. Your overall *Thrive!* strategy and actions need to be documented and agreed to by your people. Different members of your people will take on different responsibilities. For each action, designate who of your people will do what to/with whom, where, when, and with what result. Use Table 4.3a/b to document these actions and responsibilities. [See example table at end of Quick Guide.]

This is your *Thrive!* **Strategy and Action Plan**. As the strategy is executed, you strategy, actions and results should be updated.

Periodically, you and your people should assess your strategies/actions near and long term impact on near and long term surviving and thriving.

When a) your strategies and actions are not building and sustaining a thriving future and/or b) there are changes in the external world and in your people, you and your people should adjust your overall *Thrive!* **Strategy and Action Plan**.

The key is to successfully execute your strategy and actions and to build a near and long term surviving and thriving future.[17] Each and

---

[17] At this point, you should have enough good information to execute you and your people's *Thrive!* Strategy and Action Plan. If you want to develop your strategy and actions further, you may want to use more of the tools and models already mentioned and the *Thrive!* **Next Generation Toolkit**.

The full *Thrive!* **Next Generation Toolkit** includes strategy, policy and tools for creating and sustaining large, positive change and building a thriving future. You might also want to use *Thrive! - Building a Thriving Future* - a manual providing greater depth on strategy and tools and available via www.Amazon.com

all must successfully carry out the assigned action. That is, each/all must successfully do what is required to/with whoever is required, where required, when required, and with what needed/desired result.

A ***Thrive!* Strategy and Action Plan** is only as good as its successful execution and successful achievement of the desired outcome - a surviving and thriving future. *[Following is an example of a stronger **Thrive! Strategy and Action Plan** for you and your family's surviving <u>and</u> thriving future.]*

Example of you and your family surviving <u>and</u> thriving. *To build, achieve and sustain a surviving <u>and</u> thriving future, the **Thrive! Strategy and Action Plan** for you and your family and friends should be more like the following example: [Who will do what to/with whom, where, when, and with what result?]*

Starting immediately, you and your family and friends build, achieve, and sustain a surviving and thriving future, including:
- Performing well. *Starting immediately, you and your family and friends act to ensure, within the next 10 years, a) all (who are able and not appropriately retired) can work and earn a living income sufficient to survive and thrive and b) all have sufficient resources for and are living, recreating, learning so that they are surviving and thriving to maximum extent feasible.*
- Being well-off (financially). *Starting immediately, you and your family and friends act to ensure, within the next 10 years, a) all have sufficient income/resources to survive and thrive.*
- Being well nourished (food and drink). *Starting immediately, you and your family and friends act to ensure, within the next 5 years, that all have access to, be able to afford and consume healthy foods enough to survive and thrive.*
- Being well housed. *Starting immediately, you and your family and friends act to ensure, within the next 10 years, all have access to, be able to afford and live in adequate and preferably high performing housing that supports surviving and thriving.*

---

or as a free download from <u>www.ThrivingFuture.org</u>.

- Being well protected (exposures, crime). *Starting immediately, you and your family and friends act to ensure, within the next 5 years, environmental exposures in home, workplace and elsewhere are minimized so as to not prevent surviving and thriving.*
- Being well educated. *Starting immediately, you and your family and friends act to ensure, within the next 10 years, all are educated to the full extent of their abilities, needs and desires and to support their surviving and thriving.*
- Being physically and mentally well. *Starting immediately, you and your family and friends act to ensure, within the next 5 years, a) all receive the optimal health support to ensure, within the next 20 years, surviving and thriving and b) physical and mental health is optimized to best ensure surviving and thriving.*
- Personally growing/developing well. *Starting immediately, you and your family and friends act to ensure, within the next 10 years, all people are personally growing and developing to best ensure surviving and thriving.*
- Living within good habitat. *Starting immediately, you and your family and friends act to ensure, within next 20 years, a) all have access to habitat that best supports their surviving and thriving.*
- Not being vulnerable. *Starting immediately, you and your family and friends act to ensure, within the next 20 years, all, if vulnerable, are vulnerable only to the minimum extent feasible.*
- Producing personal and public goods. *Starting immediately, you and your family and friends act to ensure, within the next 10 years, all produce personal and public goods (including personal income/resources, housing, food and drink, energy, education, health, protection, personal growth and development, and habitat) so as to support surviving and thriving for all.*
- Living within a stable, positive climate. *Starting immediately, you and your family and friends act to ensure, within the next 2years, all behave so as to avoid negative impacts and support positive impacts so as to help ensure a stable, positive climate.*
- Being sustained. *Starting immediately, you and your family and friends act to ensure, within the next 5 years, all behave so as to ensure the sustainability of you and your family and friends.*

Thrive!

Chapter 5: How <u>you and your community</u> can thrive.

How to build, achieve and sustain a surviving and thriving future for you and your community.

Why you and your community <u>can.</u>

You and your community <u>can</u> have a surviving and thriving future. To get to that future, keep in mind that each community is different with a different future already beginning.[18] Whether that future appears bad or good, each community can do better. To build a better future, the *Thrive!* strategy and tools has been used successfully at the personal level and on larger scales (community, country). They can work for you and the community you care about. As they have for others, this strategy and these tools can help you and your community build, achieve and sustain a surviving and thriving future.

Thrive!
Keep in mind that we are more capable than any time in human history. We can build a thriving future by effectively and collaboratively using all available knowledge and tools, including "next generation" *Thrive!* strategy and tools. Next generation *Thrive!* is different and better than anything in human history. It is <u>achieving</u> a thriving future at each level. It understands that <u>people's behavior</u>, including yours, makes (or breaks) a thriving future. It helps people, including you, achieve the behavior that in turn achieves a thriving future at each level and for all forever.

---

[18] A community can be defined by geography (for example, a neighborhood, a region), by political boundaries (for example, a village, town, city, county, state), or by common population characteristics (e.g. racial/ethnic, gender, economics, political view, similar mission, religion, labor, profession, business).

Why you and your community <u>must</u>.

You and your community <u>must</u> have a surviving and thriving future. Each community <u>must</u> do better whether that future appears bad or good. Why? Even those communities that have a good future are not fully thriving, are not likely to be fully thriving in the future, and are still facing uncertainties about the long term future. You and your community want and need a surviving and thriving future because your community's future is endangered and because of our human need to survive and desire to thrive. What drives a community and its people is our human need to survive and desire to thrive now and in a sustainable future. Further, because your community's people (past and present) have broken some part of your community and endangered its future, you and your community's people (present and future) must help fix what is broken and build a survivable and thriving future for your community.

Why we all must and can do it together.

To build this better future, your community's people and leaders should be partners in this endeavor from the beginning and through each step. Success is dependent on positive and effective leadership from your community's leaders and people. How that leadership comes about is the subject of some debate. Some people argue for a leader driven approach where the leader creates the vision and motivation and the people join and/or follow. Some argue for bottom-up or self-organizing approaches where the people lead and the traditional leaders may or may not join and/or follow. Some argue for a collaborative approach where the traditional leaders and the people (also serving as leaders) jointly provide leadership, vision, motivation, strategy and successful execution. In general, the latter approach probably has the greater potential to create <u>and</u> sustain large, positive change and a surviving and thriving community.

Some communities will be geographic communities (including villages, towns, cities, counties and states). When feasible and when your community's governments are a positive force, governments should be part of the leadership and be partners in building a surviving and thriving community. However, it is not sufficient for governments to be the only leaders in this endeavor. Non-governmental organizations need to be leaders. Private businesses need to be leaders. Individual people need to be leaders. To be successful, this needs to be a whole community (people and leaders) endeavor.

Key to success is the strong desire by you and your community to move your community from its current vulnerabilities through and beyond surviving to a sustained thriving future.

How to build, achieve, and sustain a surviving and thriving future for you and your community.

To build a surviving and thriving future for you and your community, *Thrive!* can be helpful to you and is laid out in the following "how-to".[19] The following "how-to" is a relatively basic "how-to". The underlying principles and the strategy, models and tools apply to communities from small size and low complexity to very large size and very high complexity.

It is adapted from the *Thrive!* **Next Generation Toolkit**. It is customized to help you and your people build, achieve and sustain a surviving and thriving future. More is available in the full **People's Guide** and in *Thrive!* **- Building a Thriving Future** - a manual providing greater depth on strategy and tools and available via www.Amazon.com or free download from www.ThrivingFuture.org.

---

[19] Note that Using *Thrive!* for a community is very similar to using it for a country. If your primary interest is in a whole country, you may want to skip to the next chapter. A country is handled separately because of likely increased size and likely increased complexity and diversity of its people, its politics, its geography, its resources and its habitat.

Step 1.

Step 1. Current state of you and your community. The first major step is to understand the current state of your community.

a. What is your community? Let's first go through what is your community today. A community can be defined by geography (for example, a neighborhood, a region), by political boundaries (for example, a village, town, city, county, state), or by common population characteristics (e.g. racial/ethnic, gender, economics, political view, similar mission, religion, labor, profession, business). It can be a combination of these.

For your community, what are its geographic boundaries and characteristics? Use Table 5.1 (end of Quick Guide) to describe all of the following for your community.[20] Its gender, age, racial, ethnic make-up. Lifestyle. Type of work. Financial situation. Food and drink. Housing. Protection (crime, environmental hazards). Education. Physical and mental health. Personal growth and development. Habitat (living environment, neighboring communities, part of what state, country, continent). Producing what. Climate. Sustainability.

b. How well is your community? How well (surviving and thriving) is your community? Use Table 5.2 (end of Quick Guide) to describe how well is your community.[21] How well is your community in terms of performing well? Being well-off (financially)? Being well nourished (food and drink)? Being well housed? Being well protected (exposures, crime)? Being well educated? Being physically and mentally well? Personally growing/developing well? Living within good habitat? Not being vulnerable? Producing personal and public goods? Living within a stable, positive climate? Being sustained?

---

[20] Free download of larger, fillable worksheets at www.ThrivingFuture.org
[21] Free download of larger, fillable worksheets at www.ThrivingFuture.org

Answering "yes" to all indicates current surviving and thriving. Though the "yes" answers are good, there is still future work to make sure this continues. "No" answers are bad and mean there is current <u>and</u> future work to be done.

c. What positively or negatively impacts your community? What positively or negatively impacts or is likely to impact you and your community's surviving and thriving? Use Table 5.2 to describe all of the following impacts (positive and negative; current and future). What impacts your community's performing well? Being well-off (financially)? Being well nourished (food and drink)? Being well housed? Being well protected (exposures, crime)? Being well educated? Being physically and mentally well? Personally growing/developing well? Living within good habitat? Not being vulnerable? Producing personal and public goods? Living within a stable, positive climate? Being sustained?

Positive impacts improve and/or sustain surviving and thriving. If they will continue, you probably can focus on other things. If they may or may not continue, your action is needed to make them continue and/or to develop other things to compensate. Bad impacts prevent or limit surviving and thriving. If they will not continue, you probably can focus on other things. If they may or may not continue, your action is needed to stop them or to avoid or minimize their impact.

d. What is near and long term future behavior of your community? How is your community likely to behave in the near and long term future. For example, will it behave (individual behavior; group behavior, overall community behavior) so as to protect/improve public services, help each other survive/thrive, protect/increase jobs, maintain/improve community environment, and/or sustain the community near and long term.

Use Table 5.2 to describe all of the following behaviors. How will your community behave with respect to performing well? Being well-off (financially). Being well nourished (food and drink)? Being well housed? Being well protected (exposures, crime)?

Being well educated? Being physically and mentally well?
Personally growing/developing well? Living within good habitat?
Not being vulnerable? Producing personal and public goods?
Living within a stable, positive climate? Being sustained?

e. Want more on your community's future and behavior? At this
point, you have a baseline with which to measure progress for your
community. You have enough information to move to Step 2 and to
develop strategy for you and your community. If you want more
information before moving to strategy, you may want to use more of
the tools and models already mentioned and the *Thrive!* **Next
Generation Toolkit.**[22]

Step 2.

**Step 2. Strategy to achieve you and your community's surviving
and thriving future.** The next major step is to develop the strategy
that will help you and your community build and achieve a surviving
and thriving future.

a. What will your community be in the future? What will be your
desired and/or likely future community? Use Table 5.3 (end of
Quick Guide) to describe the likely future.[23] If there are any changes
to your community that are desired or likely, take them into account.
You may want to leave out parts of the community that should not or
will not be part of your community. You may want to include future
additions that should or will be part of the community (for example,
the next neighborhood, the next village/town/city, the surrounding
area, another interest group, another population).

---

[22] Using the full *Thrive!* **Next Generation Toolkit** is recommended because it
includes more strategy, policy and tools for creating and sustaining large, positive
change and building a surviving and thriving future. You might also want to use
Thrive! **- Building a Thriving Future** - a manual providing greater depth on
strategy and tools and available via www.Amazon.com or as free download from
www.ThrivingFuture.org.

[23] Free download of larger, fillable worksheets at www.ThrivingFuture.org

With this updated information, what will be your community's geographic boundaries and characteristics? Type of work/how people live. Financial situation. Food and drink. Housing. Protection (crime, environmental hazards). Education. Physical and mental health. Personal growth and development. Habitat (living environment, neighboring communities, part of what state, country, continent). Producing what. Climate. Sustainability. Update Table 5.3 with this information.

b. How well should your community be in the near and long term future? How well should your community as a whole be in the future? Overall, it should be <u>surviving and thriving</u>. With this as a guide, you and your community choose the surviving and thriving future your community wants to build and achieve. The *"Thrive!* strategy" will help you accomplish that.

Use Table 5.4 (end of Quick Guide) to describe how well your community should be.[24] From you and your community's view and to be surviving and thriving, indicate to what extent your community should be performing well. Be well-off (financially). Be well nourished (food and drink). Be well housed. Be well protected (exposures, crime). Be well educated. Be physically and mentally well. Be personally growing/developing well. Be living within good habitat. Not be vulnerable. Be producing personal and public goods. Be living within a stable, positive climate. Be sustained. Again, your community should be surviving and thriving.

c. What has to change externally and internally to achieve your community's thriving future? What has to change externally (outside your community) and internally (within your community) to progress from your community's current status to achieve your desired surviving and thriving status? In Step 1, you identified what positively and negatively impacts or is likely to impact your community. Update those, including any changes to your future community from Step 2a.

---

[24] Free download of larger, fillable worksheets at <u>www.ThrivingFuture.org</u>

Given those, what has to change to achieve a surviving and thriving future? Use Table 5.4 to describe all that has to change externally and internally for the following. To achieve performing well? Being well-off (financially)? Being well nourished (food and drink)? Being well housed? Being well protected (exposures, crime)? Being well educated? Being physically and mentally well? Personally growing/developing well? Living within good habitat? Not being vulnerable? Producing personal and public goods? Living within a stable, positive climate? Being sustained?

Good changes improve and/or sustain surviving and thriving. Bad changes prevent and/or limit surviving and thriving.

d. What actions by your community are needed to achieve its thriving future? What internal actions (by you and your community) and external actions (by others) are needed to bring about the needed external and internal changes (identified in "c") that improve your community's current status enough to achieve the desired surviving and thriving status? [See Figure 5.1] [25]

External actions by others. There are very important <u>external</u> actions that are needed to support the *Thrive!* strategy. You already identified what has to change externally to achieve your community's surviving and thriving future. What external actions by others will bring about the needed changes?

Use Table 5.4 to describe all the external actions to be taken.

Identify external actions by others that support <u>good</u> changes that will help improve and/or sustain surviving and thriving. If good changes are likely to occur, together with others support them. If good changes are not likely to occur, together with others support them and develop other good changes to compensate.

---

[25] An action is defined as "who will do what to/with whom, where, when, and with what result."

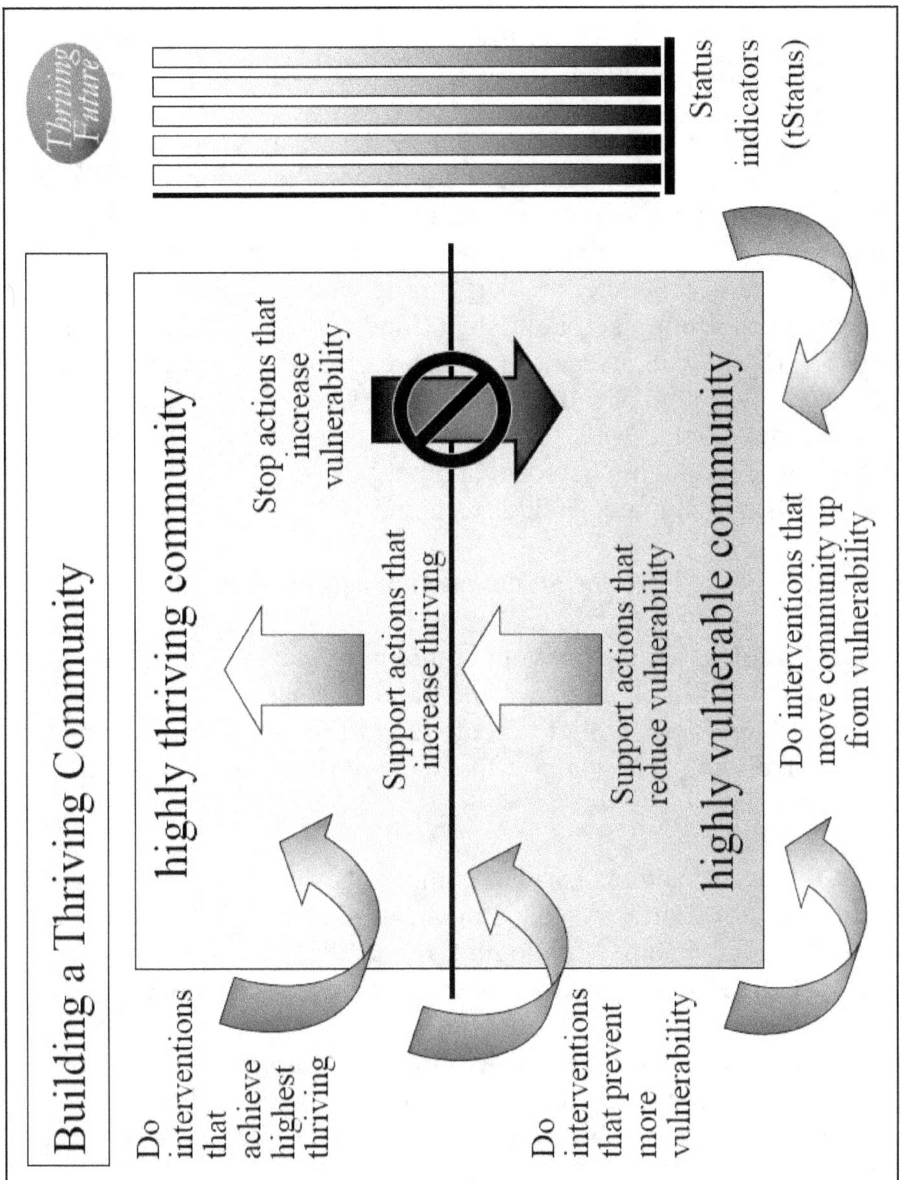

Figure 5.1. Building a Thriving Community.

Identify external actions by others that stop <u>bad</u> changes that prevent or limit surviving and thriving. If bad changes are not likely to occur, together with others ensure they do not. If bad changes are likely to occur, together with others change them, stop them or avoid/reduce their impact.

Internal actions by your community. There are very important <u>internal</u> actions by you and your community that support the *Thrive!* strategy. Individual community members and your community as a whole should support your strategy to ensure your community and each community member are performing well. Being well-off (financially). Being well nourished (food and drink). Being well housed. Being well protected (exposures, crime). Being well educated. Being physically and mentally well. Personally growing/developing well. Living within good habitat. Not being vulnerable. Producing personal and public goods. Living within a stable, positive climate. Being sustained.

Use Table 5.4 to describe all the internal actions to be taken.

Identify internal actions by your community that support <u>good</u> changes that will help improve and/or sustain surviving and thriving. If good changes are likely to occur, support them. If good changes are not likely to occur, support them and develop other good changes to compensate.

Identify internal actions by your community that stop <u>bad</u> changes that prevent or limit surviving and thriving. If bad changes are not likely to occur, ensure they do not. If bad changes are likely to occur, change them, stop them or avoid/reduce their impact.

e. Overall *Thrive!* strategy and actions. Your overall *Thrive!* strategy and actions need to be documented and agreed to by your community. This will be your community's *Thrive!* **Strategy and Action Plan.** Different members of your community will take on different responsibilities. For each action, designate who of your community will do what to/with whom, where, when, and with what result. Use Table 5.4 to document these actions and responsibilities. [See example table at end of Quick Guide.] Make sure you have all the actions that are needed to build, achieve and sustain a surviving and thriving community.

As the strategy is executed, you strategy, actions and results should be updated in your *Thrive!* **Strategy and Action Plan**.

Periodically, you and your community should do an evaluation - assessing your strategies/actions near and long term impact on near and long term surviving and thriving. When a) your strategies and actions are not building and sustaining a thriving future and/or b) there are changes in the external world and in your community, you and your community should adjust your overall *Thrive!* **Strategy and Action Plan**.

The key is to successfully execute your community's *Thrive!* **Strategy and Action Plan** and to build a near and long term surviving and thriving future.[26] Each and all must successfully carry out the assigned action. That is, each/all must successfully do what is required to/with whoever is required, where required, when required, and with what needed/desired result. A *Thrive!* **Strategy and Action Plan** is only as good as its successful execution and successful achievement of the desired outcome - a surviving and thriving future. *[Following is an example of a stronger* **Thrive!** *Strategy and Action Plan for you and your community's surviving and thriving future.]*

---

[26] At this point, you may have enough good information to execute you and your country's *Thrive!* strategy and actions. If you want to develop your strategy and actions further, you may want to use more of the tools and models already mentioned and the *Thrive!* **Next Generation Toolkit**.

The full *Thrive!* **Next Generation Toolkit** (Appendix) includes strategy, policy and tools for creating and sustaining large, positive change and building a thriving future. Your community might also want to use *Thrive! - **Building a Thriving Future** - a manual providing greater depth on strategy and tools and available via www.Amazon.com or free download from www.ThrivingFuture.org.

Example of you and your community surviving <u>and</u> thriving. *To build, achieve and sustain a surviving <u>and</u> thriving future, the **Thrive! Strategy and Action Plan** for you and your community should be more like the following example: [Who will do what to/with whom, where, when, and with what result?]*

Starting immediately for you and your community, people, business/industry, private organizations (local, country), governments (local, country) and international organizations) build, achieve, and sustain a surviving and thriving future for you and your community, including:[27]

- Performing well. *Starting immediately for you and your community, people, business/industry, private organizations (local, country), governments (local, country) and international organizations act to ensure, within the next 10 years, a) all (who are able and not appropriately retired) can work and earn a living income sufficient to survive and thrive and b) all have sufficient resources for and are living, recreating, learning so that they are surviving and thriving to maximum extent feasible.*
- Being well-off (financially). *Starting immediately for you and your community, people, business/industry, private organizations (local, country), governments (local, country) and international organizations act to ensure, within the next 10 years, a) all have sufficient income/resources to survive and thrive and b) all governments have sufficient resources to provide needed (supporting surviving) and desired (supporting thriving) public programs and policies.*
- Being well nourished (food and drink). *Starting immediately for you and your community, people, business/industry, private organizations (local, country), governments (local, country) and international organizations act to ensure, within the next 10 years, that all have access to, be able to afford and consume healthy foods enough to survive and thrive.*
- Being well housed. *Starting immediately for you and your community, people, business/industry, private organizations (local,*

---

[27] International organizations could be a major resource, especially if the community extends beyond a single country's boundaries.

country), governments (local, country) and international organizations act to ensure, within the next 20 years, all have access to, be able to afford and live in adequate and preferably high performing housing that supports surviving and thriving.

- Being well protected (exposures, crime). *Starting immediately for you and your community, people, business/industry, private organizations (local, country), governments (local, country) and international organizations act to ensure, within the next 10 years, a) environmental exposures in home, workplace and elsewhere are minimized so as to not prevent surviving and thriving and b) crimes are minimized to the extent feasible in terms of frequency and impact so as to not prevent surviving and thriving.*

- Being well educated. *Starting immediately for you and your community, people, business/industry, private organizations (local, country), governments (local, country) and international organizations act to ensure, within the next 20 years, all are educated to the full extent of their abilities, needs and desires and to support their surviving and thriving.*

- Being physically and mentally well. *Starting immediately for you and your community, people, business/industry, private organizations (local, country), governments (local, country) and international organizations act to ensure, within the next 20 years, a) all receive the optimal health support to ensure, within the next 10 years, surviving and thriving and b) physical and mental health is optimized to best ensure surviving and thriving.*

- Personally growing/developing well. *Starting immediately for you and your community, people, business/industry, private organizations (local, country), governments (local, country) and international organizations act to ensure, within the next 10 years, all are personally growing and developing to best ensure surviving and thriving.*

- Living within good habitat. *Starting immediately for you and your community, people, business/industry, private organizations (local, country), governments (local, country) and international organizations act to ensure, within the next 10 years, a) all have access to habitat that best supports their surviving and thriving and b) your community has the optimal mix, quantity and quality of habitat to best support its inhabitants' surviving and thriving.*

- Not being vulnerable. *Starting immediately for you and your community, people, business/industry, private organizations (local, country), governments (local, country) and international organizations act to ensure, within the next 10 years, that all, if vulnerable, are vulnerable only to the minimum extent feasible.*

- Producing personal and public goods. *Starting immediately for you and your community, people, business/industry, private organizations (local, country), governments (local, country) and international organizations act to ensure, within the next 10 years, your community produces personal and public goods (including personal income/resources, housing, food and drink, energy, education, health, protection, personal growth and development, and habitat) so as to support surviving and thriving for all.*

- Living within a stable, positive climate. *Starting immediately for you and your community, people, business/industry, private organizations (local, country), governments (local, country) and international organizations act to ensure, within the next 10 years, all behave so as to avoid negative impacts and support positive impacts so as to help ensure a stable, positive climate.*

- Being sustained. *Starting immediately for you and your community, people, business/industry, private organizations (local, country), governments (local, country) and international organizations act to ensure, within the next 5 years, all people behave so as to ensure the sustainability of your community and its people.*

Chapter 6: How <u>you and your country</u> can thrive.

How to build, achieve and sustain a surviving and thriving future for you and your country.

Why you and your country <u>can</u>.

You and your country can have a surviving and thriving future. To get to that future, keep in mind that each country is different with a different future already beginning. Whether that future appears bad or good, each country can do better. To build a better future, the *Thrive!* strategy and tools has been used successfully at the personal level and on larger scales (community, country). They can work for you and the country you care about. As they have for others, this strategy and these tools can help you and your country build, achieve and sustain a surviving and thriving future.

Thrive!
Keep in mind that we are more capable than any time in human history. We can build a thriving future by effectively and collaboratively using all available knowledge and tools, including "next generation" *Thrive!* strategy and tools. Next generation *Thrive!* is different and better than anything in human history. It is <u>achieving</u> a thriving future at each level. It understands that <u>people's behavior</u>, including yours, makes (or breaks) a thriving future. It helps people, including you, achieve the behavior that in turn achieves a thriving future at each level and for all forever.

Why you and your country <u>must</u>.

You and your country <u>must</u> have a surviving and thriving future. Each country <u>must</u> do better whether that future appears bad or good. Why? Even those countries that have a good future are not fully thriving, are not likely to be fully thriving in the future, and are still facing uncertainties about the long term future. You and your country want and need a surviving and thriving future because your country's future is endangered and because of our human need to survive and desire to thrive. What drives your country and its people is our human need to survive and desire to thrive now and in a sustainable future. Further, because your country's people (past and present) have broken some part of your country and endangered its future, you and your country's people (present and future) must help fix what is broken and build a survivable and thriving future for your country.

Why we all must and can do it together.

To build this better future, your country's people and leadership should be partners in this endeavor from the beginning and through each step. Success is dependent on positive leadership from the country's people and leaders. How that leadership comes about is the subject of some debate. Some people argue for a leader driven approach where the leader creates the vision and motivation and the people join and/or follow. Some argue for bottom-up or self-organizing approaches where the people lead and the traditional leaders may or may not join and/or follow. Some argue for a collaborative approach where the traditional leaders and the people (also serving as leaders) jointly provide leadership, vision, motivation, strategy and successful execution. In general, the latter approach probably has the greater potential to create <u>and</u> sustain large, positive change and a surviving and thriving country.

When feasible and when your country's national, state and local governments are a positive force, your governments should be part of the leadership and be partners in building a surviving and thriving country. However, it is not sufficient for government to be the only leader in this endeavor. Non-governmental organizations need to be leaders. Private businesses need to be leaders. Individual people need to be leaders. To be successful, this needs to be a whole country (people and leaders) endeavor.

Key to success is the strong desire by you and your country's people to move your country from its current vulnerabilities through and beyond surviving to a sustained thriving future.

How to build, achieve, and sustain a surviving and thriving future for you and your country.

To build a surviving and thriving future for you and your country, *Thrive!* can be helpful to you and is laid out in the following "how-to".[28] The strategy, models and tools apply to countries from small size and low complexity to very large size and very high complexity.

The following "how-to", by design, is simple but powerful. It is a relatively basic how-to providing the framework if not necessarily all the details for doing "your country" strategy.

This "your country" how-to is adapted from the *Thrive!* **Next Generation Toolkit**. More is available in the full **People's Guide** and in *Thrive!* **- Building a Thriving Future** - a manual providing greater depth on strategy and tools and available via www.Amazon.com or free download from www.ThrivingFuture.org. The optimal approach is to use the following how-to framework and also use the strategies, models and tools in the full **People's Guide** and in *Thrive!* **- Building a Thriving Future**.

---

[28] Note that using *Thrive!* for a country is very similar to using it for a community. In many ways, a country is a community. Here a country is handled separately because of the likely increased size, larger number of governments, and the likely increased complexity and diversity of its people, its politics, its geography, its resources and its habitat.

Step 1.

Step 1. Current state of you and your country. The first major step is to understand the current state of your country.

a. What is your country? Let's first go through what is your country today. A country is defined by its geography, political boundaries, or population characteristics (e.g. racial/ethnic, gender, economics, political view, similar mission, religion, labor, profession, business).

For your country, what are its geographic boundaries and characteristics? Use Table 6.1 (end of Quick Guide) to describe all of the following for your country.[29] Its gender, age, racial, ethnic make-up. Lifestyle. Type of work. Financial situation. Food and drink. Housing. Protection (crime, environmental hazards). Education. Physical and mental health. Personal growth and development. Habitat (living environment, neighboring communities, part of what state, country, continent). Producing what. Climate. Sustainability.

b. How well is your country? How well (surviving and thriving) is your country? Use Table 6.2 (end of Quick Guide) to describe how well is your country.[30] How well is your country in terms of performing well? Being well-off (financially)? Being well nourished (food and drink)? Being well housed? Being well protected (exposures, crime)? Being well educated? Being physically and mentally well? Personally growing/developing well? Living within good habitat? Not being vulnerable? Producing personal and public goods? Living within a stable, positive climate? Being sustained?

Answering "yes" to all indicates current surviving and thriving. Though the "yes" answers are good, there is still future work to

---

[29] Free download of larger, fillable worksheets at www.ThrivingFuture.org
[30] Free download of larger, fillable worksheets at www.ThrivingFuture.org

make sure this continues. "No" answers are bad and mean there is current and future work to be done.

c. What positively or negatively impacts your country? What positively or negatively impacts or is likely to impact you and your country's surviving and thriving? Use Table 6.2 to describe all of the following impacts (positive and negative; current and future). What impacts your country's performing well? Being well-off (financially)? Being well nourished (food and drink)? Being well housed? Being well protected (exposures, crime)? Being well educated? Being physically and mentally well? Personally growing/developing well? Living within good habitat? Not being vulnerable? Producing personal and public goods? Living within a stable, positive climate? Being sustained?

Positive impacts improve and/or sustain surviving and thriving. If they will continue, you probably can focus on other things. If they may or may not continue, your action is needed to make them continue and/or to develop other things to compensate. Bad impacts prevent or limit surviving and thriving. If they will not continue, you probably can focus on other things. If they may or may not continue, your action is needed to stop them or to avoid or minimize their impact.

d. What is near and long term future behavior of your country? How is your country likely to behave in the near and long term future. For example, will it behave (individual behavior; group behavior, overall country behavior) so as to protect/improve public services, help each other survive/thrive, protect/increase jobs, maintain/improve country's environment, and/or sustain the country near and long term.

Use Table 6.2 to describe all of the following behaviors. How will your country behave with respect to performing well? Being well-off (financially). Being well nourished (food and drink)? Being well housed? Being well protected (exposures, crime)? Being well educated? Being physically and mentally well? Personally growing/developing well? Living within good habitat? Not being vulnerable? Producing personal and public goods? Living within a stable, positive climate? Being sustained?

e. Want more on your country's future and behavior? At this point, you have a basic baseline with which to measure progress for your country. Your country may have enough good information to move to Step 2 and to develop strategy for you and your country. If your country wants more information before moving to strategy, your country may want to use more of the tools and models already mentioned and the *Thrive!* **Next Generation Toolkit**. This is encouraged and may be necessary for very large, complex countries.

Using the full *Thrive!* **Next Generation Toolkit** is recommended because it includes more strategy, policy and tools for creating and sustaining large, positive change and building a surviving and thriving future. Using the manual ***Thrive!* - Building a Thriving Future** is recommended because it provides even greater depth on strategy and tools. It is available via www.amazon.com or free download from www.ThrivingFuture.org.

Step 2.

Step 2. Strategy to achieve you and your country's surviving and thriving future. The next major step is to develop the strategy that will help you and your country build and achieve a surviving and thriving future.

a. What will your country be in the future? What will be your likely future country? Use Table 6.3 (end of Quick Guide) to describe the likely future.[31] If there are any changes to your country that are desired or likely, take them into account. What will be its characteristics? Type of work/how people live. Financial situation. Food and drink. Housing. Protection (crime, environmental hazards). Education. Physical and mental health. Personal growth and development. Habitat (living environment, neighboring

---

[31] Free download of larger, fillable worksheets at www.ThrivingFuture.org

communities, part of what state, country, continent). Producing what. Climate. Sustainability.

b. How well should your country be in the near and long term future? How well should your country as a whole be in the future? Overall, it should be <u>surviving and thriving</u>. With this as a guide, you and your country choose the surviving and thriving future your community wants to build and achieve. The "*Thrive!* strategy" will help you accomplish that.

Use Table 6.4 (end of Quick Guide) to describe how well your country should be.[32] From you and your country's view and to be surviving and thriving, indicate to what extent your country should be performing well. Be well-off (financially). Be well nourished (food and drink). Be well housed. Be well protected (exposures, crime). Be well educated. Be physically and mentally well. Be personally growing/developing well. Be living within good habitat. Not be vulnerable. Be producing personal and public goods. Be living within a stable, positive climate. Be sustained. Again, your country should be surviving and thriving.

c. What has to change externally and internally to achieve your country's thriving future? What has to change externally (outside your country) and internally (within your country) to progress from your country's current status to achieve your desired surviving and thriving status? In Step 1, you identified what positively and negatively impacts or is likely to impact your country. Update those, including any changes to your future country.

Given those, what has to change externally and internally to achieve a surviving and thriving future? Use Table 6.4 to describe all that has to change for the following. To achieve performing well? Being well-off (financially)? Being well nourished (food and drink)? Being well housed? Being well protected (exposures, crime)? Being well educated? Being physically and mentally well? Personally growing/developing well? Living within good habitat?

---

[32] Free download of larger, fillable worksheets at <u>www.ThrivingFuture.org</u>

Not being vulnerable? Producing personal and public goods?
Living within a stable, positive climate? Being sustained?

Good changes improve and/or sustain surviving and thriving. Bad
changes prevent and/or limit surviving and thriving.

**d. What actions by your country are needed to achieve its
thriving future?** What internal actions (by you and your country)
and external actions (by others) are needed to bring about the needed
external and internal changes (identified in "c") that improve your
country's current status enough to achieve the desired surviving and
thriving status? [Figure 6.1] [33]

External actions by others. There are very important <u>external</u>
actions that are needed to support the *Thrive!* strategy. You already
identified what has to change externally to achieve your country's
surviving and thriving future. What external actions by others will
bring about the needed changes?

Use Table 6.4 to describe all the external actions to be taken.

Identify external actions by others that support <u>good</u> changes that
will help improve and/or sustain surviving and thriving. If good
changes are likely to occur, together with others support them. If
good changes are not likely to occur, together with others support
them and develop other good changes to compensate. [Use Table
6.4]

Identify external actions by others that stop <u>bad</u> changes that prevent
or limit surviving and thriving. If bad changes are not likely to
occur, together with others ensure they do not. If bad changes are
likely to occur, together with others change them, stop them or
avoid/reduce their impact.

---

[33] An action is defined as "who will do what to/with whom, where, when, and with
what result."

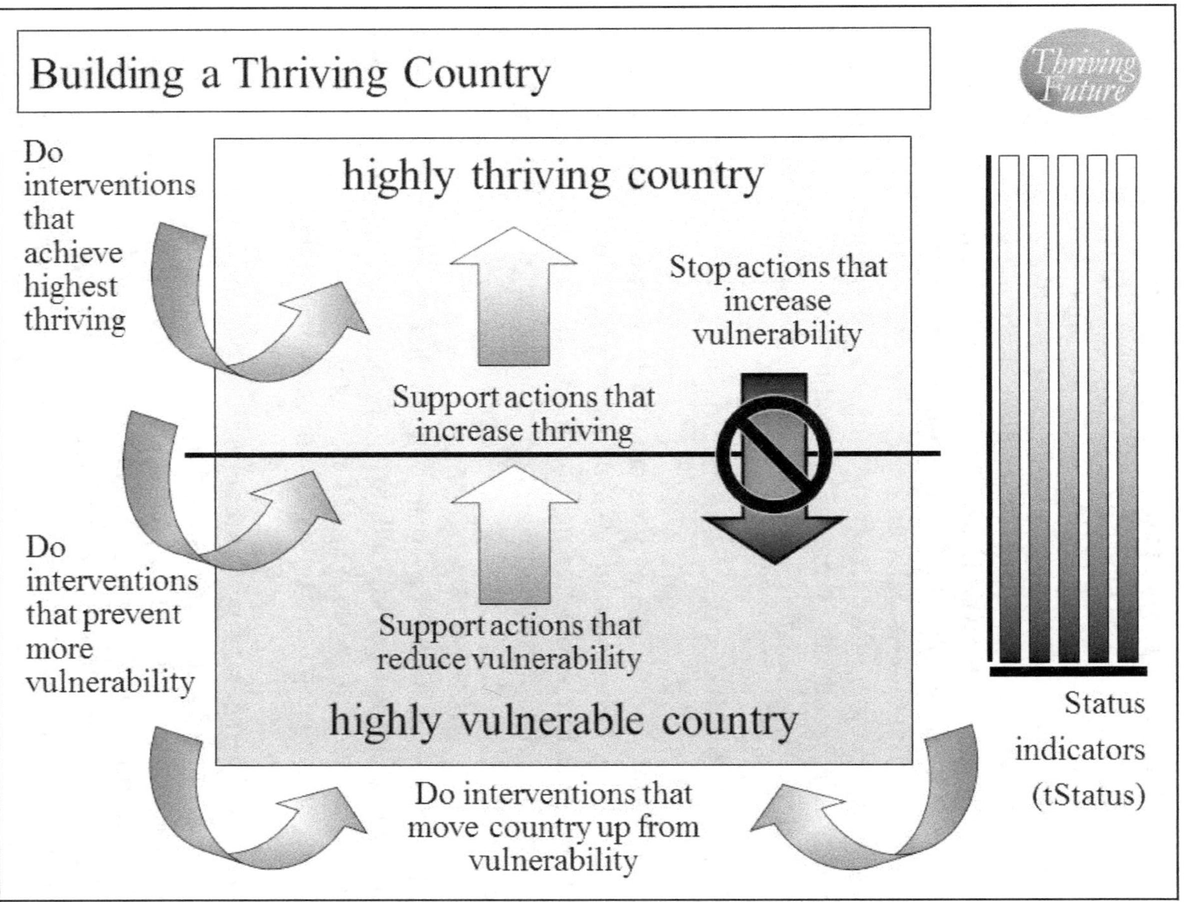

Figure 6.1. Building a Thriving Country.

Internal actions by your country. There are very important <u>internal</u> actions by you and your country that support the *Thrive!* strategy. Individual country members and your country as a whole should support your country's strategy to ensure your country and each country member are performing well. Being well-off (financially). Being well nourished (food and drink). Being well housed. Being well protected (exposures, crime). Being well educated. Being physically and mentally well. Personally growing/developing well. Living within good habitat. Not being vulnerable. Producing personal and public goods. Living within a stable, positive climate. Being sustained.

Use Table 6.4 to describe all the internal actions to be taken.

Identify internal actions by your country that support <u>good</u> changes that will help improve and/or sustain surviving and thriving. If good changes are likely to occur, support them. If good changes are not likely to occur, support them and develop other good changes to compensate.

Identify internal actions by your country that stop <u>bad</u> changes that prevent or limit surviving and thriving. If bad changes are not likely to occur, ensure they do not. If bad changes are likely to occur, change them, stop them or avoid/reduce their impact.

Overall *Thrive!* strategy and actions. Your country's overall *Thrive!* strategy and actions need to be documented and agreed to by your country. This will be your country's *Thrive!* **Strategy and Action Plan**. Different members of your country will take on different responsibilities. For each action, designate who of your country will do what to/with whom, where, when, and with what result. Use Table 6.4 to document these actions and responsibilities. [See example table at end of Quick Guide.] Make sure your country has all the actions that are needed to build, achieve and sustain a surviving and thriving country.

Thrive!

As the strategy is executed, your country's strategy, actions and results should be updated in your ***Thrive!* Strategy and Action Plan**.

Periodically, you and your country should do an evaluation - assessing your country's strategies/actions near and long term impact on near and long term surviving and thriving. When a) your country's strategies and actions are not building and sustaining a thriving future and/or b) there are changes in the external world and in your country, you and your country should adjust your overall ***Thrive!*** strategy and actions.

The key is to successfully execute your country's ***Thrive!* Strategy and Action Plan** and to build a near and long term surviving and thriving future.[34] Each and all must successfully carry out the assigned action. That is, each/all must successfully do what is required to/with whoever is required, where required, when required, and with what needed/desired result. A ***Thrive!* Strategy and Action Plan** is only as good as its successful execution and successful achievement of the desired outcome - a surviving and thriving future. *[Following is an example of a stronger **Thrive! Strategy and Action Plan** for you and your country's surviving <u>and</u> thriving future.]*

---

[34] At this point, you and your country should have enough good information to execute you and your country's ***Thrive!*** Strategy and Action Plan. If you and your country want to develop strategy and actions further, you and your country may want to use more of the tools and models already mentioned and the ***Thrive!* Next Generation Toolkit.** This is encouraged and may be necessary for very large, complex countries.

   As stated earlier, this "how-to", by design, is simple but powerful. It is relatively basic providing the framework for doing "your country" strategy. The optimal approach is to use this how-to framework <u>and</u> use the more extensive strategy, models and tools in a) the ***Thrive!* Next Generation Toolkit** and b) ***Thrive! - Building a Thriving Future*** available via <u>www.Amazon.com</u> or free download from <u>www.ThrivingFuture.org</u>.

Example of you and your country surviving <u>and</u> thriving. *To build, achieve and sustain a surviving <u>and</u> thriving future, the **Thrive! Strategy and Action Plan** for you and your country should be more like the following example: [Who will do what to/with whom, where, when, and with what result?]*

Starting immediately for you and your country, people, business/industry, private organizations (local, country), governments (local, country) and international organizations build, achieve, and sustain a surviving and thriving future for you and your country, including:

- Performing well. *Starting immediately for you and your country, people, business/industry, private organizations (local, country), governments (local, country) and international organizations act to ensure, within the next 20 years, a) all (who are able and not appropriately retired) can work and earn a living income sufficient to survive and thrive and b) all have sufficient resources for and are living, recreating, learning so that they are surviving and thriving to maximum extent feasible.*

- Being well-off (financially). *Starting immediately for you and your country, people, business/industry, private organizations (local, country), governments (local, country) and international organizations act to ensure, within the next 20 years, a) all have sufficient income/resources to survive and thrive and b) all governments have sufficient resources to provide needed (supporting surviving) and desired (supporting thriving) public programs and policies.*

- Being well nourished (food and drink). *Starting immediately for you and your country, people, business/industry, private organizations (local, country), governments (local, country) and international organizations act to ensure, within the next 20 years, that all have access to, be able to afford and consume healthy foods enough to survive and thrive.*

- Being well housed. *Starting immediately for you and your country, people, business/industry, private organizations (local, country), governments (local, country) and international organizations act to ensure, within the next 20 years, all have access to, be able to afford and live in adequate and preferably high performing housing that supports surviving and thriving.*

- Being well protected (exposures, crime). *Starting immediately for you and your country, people, business/industry, private organizations (local, country), governments (local, country) and international organizations act to ensure, within the next 20 years, a) environmental exposures in home, workplace and elsewhere are minimized so as to not prevent surviving and thriving and b) crimes are minimized to the extent feasible in terms of frequency and impact so as to not prevent surviving and thriving.*

- Being well educated. *Starting immediately for you and your country, people, business/industry, private organizations (local, country), governments (local, country) and international organizations act to ensure, within the next 20 years, all people are educated to the full extent of their abilities, needs and desires and to support their surviving and thriving.*

- Being physically and mentally well. *Starting immediately for you and your country, people, business/industry, private organizations (local, country), governments (local, country) and international organizations act to ensure, within the next 20 years, a) all receive the optimal health support to ensure, within the next 20 years, surviving and thriving and b) physical and mental health is optimized to best ensure surviving and thriving.*

- Personally growing/developing well. *Starting immediately for you and your country, people, business/industry, private organizations (local, country), governments (local, country) and international organizations act to ensure, within the next 20 years, all are personally growing and developing to best ensure surviving and thriving.*

- Living within good habitat. *Starting immediately for you and your country, people, business/industry, private organizations (local, country), governments (local, country) and international organizations act to ensure, within the next 20 years, a) all have access to habitat that best supports their surviving and thriving and b) your country has the optimal mix, quantity and quality of habitat to best support its inhabitants' surviving and thriving.*

- Not being vulnerable. *Starting immediately for you and your country, people, business/industry, private organizations (local, country), governments (local, country) and international organizations act to ensure, within the next 20 years, your country and all of its people, if vulnerable, are vulnerable only to the minimum extent feasible.*

- Producing personal and public goods. *Starting immediately for you and your country, people, business/industry, private organizations (local, country), governments (local, country) and international organizations act to ensure, within the next 20 years, your country produces personal and public goods (including personal income/resources, housing, food and drink, energy, education, health, protection, personal growth and development, and habitat) so as to support surviving and thriving for all persons and for our world overall.*

- Living within a stable, positive climate. *Starting immediately for you and your country, people, business/industry, private organizations (local, country), governments (local, country) and international organizations act to ensure, within the next 10 years, all behave so as to avoid negative impacts and support positive impacts so as to help ensure a stable, positive climate.*

- Being sustained. *Starting immediately for you and your country, people, business/industry, private organizations (local, country), governments (local, country) and international organizations act to ensure, within the next 5 years, all behave so as to ensure the sustainability of your country _and_ its people.*

Chapter 7: How <u>our world</u> can thrive.

How to build, achieve and sustain a surviving and thriving future for our world. [35,36]

Why our world <u>can</u>.
Our world can have a surviving and thriving future. To get to that future, keep in mind that our world has a future already beginning. Whether that future appears bad or good, our world can do better. To build a better future, the *Thrive!* strategy and tools has been used successfully at the personal level and on larger scales (community, country). They can work for the world we all care about. As they have for others, this strategy and these tools can help our world build, achieve and sustain a surviving and thriving future.

Thrive!
Keep in mind that we are more capable than any time in human history. We can build a thriving future by effectively and collaboratively using all available knowledge and tools, including "next generation" *Thrive!* strategy and tools. Next generation *Thrive!* is different and better than anything in human history. It is <u>achieving</u> a thriving future at each level. It understands that <u>people's behavior</u>, including yours, makes (or breaks) a thriving future. It helps people, including you, achieve the behavior that in turn achieves a thriving future at each level and for all forever.

---

[35] In working through "how our world can thrive", the focus shifts from "you and family, friends, community and country" to "we" and "our world" in keeping with the all inclusive context. Also, in this context, the word "we" means essentially all of us, including future generations, joined together.

[36] We must keep in mind that "our world" is expanding as we explore and move beyond earth to other parts of our universe. For that reason, "a thriving future for all forever" reaches at least as far as we touch or ever hope to touch.

Thrive!

Why our world <u>must</u>.

Our world <u>must</u> have a surviving and thriving future. Our world <u>must</u> do better whether that future appears bad or good. Why? Even if we believe that our world has a good future, we are not fully thriving, are not likely to be fully thriving in the future, and are still facing uncertainties about the long term future. We want and need a surviving and thriving future because our world's future is endangered and because of our human need to survive and desire to thrive. What drives our world and all of us is our human need to survive and desire to thrive now and in a sustainable future. Further, because we (past and present) have broken parts of our world and endangered its future, we (present and future) must help fix what is broken and build a survivable and thriving future for our world.

Why we all must and can do it together.

To build this better future, we (our world's current and future people and leadership) should be partners in this endeavor from the beginning and through each step. Success is dependent on positive leadership from us - our world's people and leaders. How that leadership comes about is the subject of some debate. Some people argue for a leader driven approach where the leader creates the vision and motivation and the people join and/or follow. Some argue for bottom-up or self-organizing approaches where the people lead and the traditional leaders may or may not join and/or follow. Some argue for a collaborative approach where the traditional leaders and the people (also serving as leaders) jointly provide leadership, vision, motivation, strategy and successful execution. In general, the latter approach probably has the greater potential to create <u>and</u> sustain large, positive change and a surviving and thriving world.

For a world or global endeavor, international organizations (e.g. the United Nations, multi-country regional organizations) and country governments should be part of the leadership and be partners in building a surviving and thriving world. However, it is not sufficient for government-based international organizations and country governments to be the only leaders in this endeavor. Non-governmental international and national organizations need to be leaders. Private businesses need to be leaders. Individual people need to be leaders. To be successful, this needs to be a whole world (people and leaders) endeavor.

Key to success is the strong desire by all of us (our world's leaders and people) to move our world from its current vulnerabilities through and beyond surviving to a sustained thriving future.

How to build, achieve, and sustain a surviving and thriving future for our world.

To build a surviving and thriving future for our world, *Thrive!* can be helpful and is laid out in the following "how-to".[37]

The following "how-to", by design, is simple but powerful. It is a relatively basic how-to providing the framework, but not all the details, for doing "our world" strategy.

This "our world" how-to is adapted from the *Thrive!* **Next Generation Toolkit**. More is available in the full **People's Guide** and in *Thrive!* **- Building a Thriving Future** - a manual providing greater depth on strategy and tools and available via www.Amazon.com or free download from www.ThrivingFuture.org. The optimal approach is to use the following how-to framework and also use the strategies, models and tools in the full **People's Guide** and in *Thrive!* **- Building a Thriving Future**.

---

[37] Note that using *Thrive!* for our world has some similarities to using it for your community or your country. Our world has some of the characteristics of a community and a country but is much, much larger in terms of land/water, people, and governments and is much, much more complex and diverse in terms of its people, its politics, its geography, its resources and its habitat.

Step 1.

Step 1. Current state of our world. The first major step for us is to understand the current state of our world.

a. What is our world? We first define and understand what our world is today. Our world is defined by its geography, political boundaries, and population characteristics (including racial/ethnic, gender, economics, political view, religion, labor, profession, business).

We need to understand our world's geographic boundaries and characteristics. Use Table 7.1 (end of Quick Guide) to describe all of the following for our world.[38] Its gender, age, racial, ethnic make-up. Lifestyle. Type of work. Financial situation. Food and drink. Housing. Protection (crime, environmental hazards). Education. Physical and mental health. Personal growth and development. Habitat (living environment). Producing what. Climate. Sustainability.

b. How well is our world? How well (surviving and thriving) is our world? How well is our world in terms of performing well? Being well-off (financially)? Being well nourished (food and drink)? Being well housed? Being well protected (exposures, crime)? Being well educated? Being physically and mentally well? Personally growing/developing well? Living within good habitat? Not being vulnerable? Producing personal and public goods? Living within a stable, positive climate? Being sustained?

Answering "yes" indicates current surviving and thriving. Though the "yes" answers are good, there is still future work to make sure this continues. "No" answers are bad and mean there is current and future work to be done.

For our world, there are relatively few "yes" answers when it comes to thriving and very many no answers when it comes to surviving.

---

[38] Free download of larger, fillable worksheets at www.ThrivingFuture.org

Use Table 7.2 (end of Quick Guide) to more specifically describe how well is our world.[39]

c. What positively or negatively impacts our world? What positively or negatively impacts or is likely to impact our world's surviving and thriving? Use Table 7.2 to describe all of the following impacts (positive and negative; current and future). What impacts our world's performing well? Being well-off (financially)? Being well nourished (food and drink)? Being well housed? Being well protected (exposures, crime)? Being well educated? Being physically and mentally well? Personally growing/developing well? Living within good habitat? Not being vulnerable? Producing personal and public goods? Living within a stable, positive climate? Being sustained?

Positive impacts improve and/or sustain surviving and thriving. If they will continue, we probably can focus on other things. If they may or may not continue, our action is needed to make them continue and/or to develop other things to compensate. Bad impacts prevent or limit surviving and thriving. If they will not continue, we probably can focus on other things. If they may or may not continue, our action is needed to stop them or to avoid or minimize their impact.

d. What is near and long term future behavior of our world? How is our world (including international and country organizations, countries, business/industry, people) likely to behave in the near and long term future. For example, will it behave (individual behavior; group behavior, country behavior, overall world behavior) so as to protect/improve public services, help each other survive/thrive, protect/increase jobs, maintain/improve world's environment, and/or sustain the world near and long term.

Use Table 7.2 to describe all of the following behaviors. How will our world behave with respect to performing well? Being well-off

---

[39] Free download of larger, fillable worksheets at www.ThrivingFuture.org

(financially). Being well nourished (food and drink)? Being well housed? Being well protected (exposures, crime)? Being well educated? Being physically and mentally well? Personally growing/developing well? Living within good habitat? Not being vulnerable? Producing personal and public goods? Living within a stable, positive climate? Being sustained?

e. More on our world's future and behavior? At this point, we have a basic baseline with which to measure progress for our world. We may have enough good information to move to Step 2 and to develop strategy for our world. But using more of the tools and models already mentioned would greatly improve our chances of success and our outcome in terms of surviving and thriving.

Using the full *Thrive!* **Next Generation Toolkit** is very highly recommended because it includes more strategy, policy and tools for creating and sustaining large, positive change and building a surviving and thriving future. Using *Thrive!* **- Building a Thriving Future** is very highly recommended because it provides much greater depth on strategy and. It is available via www.Amazon.com or free download from www.ThrivingFuture.org.

Step 2.

Step 2. Strategy to achieve our world's surviving and thriving future. The next major step is to develop the strategy that will help us build and achieve a surviving and thriving future.

a. What will our world be in the future? What will be our likely future world? Population characteristics. Type of work/how people live. Financial situation. Food and drink. Housing. Protection (crime, environmental hazards). Education. Physical and mental health. Personal growth and development. Habitat (living environment, neighboring communities, part of what state, country, continent). Producing what. Climate. Sustainability.

If there are any changes to our world that are desired or likely, take them into account. Use Table 7.3 (end of Quick Guide) to describe the likely future.[40]

b. How well should our world be in the near and long term future? How well should our world as a whole be in the future? Overall, it should be <u>surviving and thriving</u>. The "*Thrive!* strategy" will help us accomplish that.

Use Table 7.4 (end of Quick Guide) to describe how well our world should be.[41] From our world's view and to be surviving and thriving, indicate to what extent our world should be performing well. Be well-off (financially). Be well nourished (food and drink). Be well housed. Be well protected (exposures, crime). Be well educated. Be physically and mentally well. Be personally growing/developing well. Be living within good habitat. Not be vulnerable. Be producing personal and public goods. Be living within a stable, positive climate. Be sustained. Again, our world should be surviving and thriving.

c. What has to change to achieve our world's thriving future? What has to change to progress from our world's current status to achieve our desired surviving and thriving status? In Step 1, we identified what positively and negatively impacts or is likely to impact our world. We include any changes to our future world.

Given those, what has to change to achieve a surviving and thriving future? To achieve performing well? Being well-off (financially)? Being well nourished (food and drink)? Being well housed? Being well protected (exposures, crime)? Being well educated? Being physically and mentally well? Personally growing/developing well? Living within good habitat? Not being vulnerable? Producing personal and public goods? Living within a stable, positive climate? Being sustained?

---

[40] Free download of larger, fillable worksheets at <u>www.ThrivingFuture.org</u>
[41] Free download of larger, fillable worksheets at <u>www.ThrivingFuture.org</u>

Good changes improve and/or sustain surviving and thriving. Bad changes prevent and/or limit surviving and thriving.

These should be the overarching changes:
- Our world and our people should be performing (living, working, recreating, learning) well enough to survive and thrive.
- Our world and our people should be well-off (financially) enough to survive and thrive.
- Our world and our people should be well nourished (food and drink) enough to survive and thrive.
- Our world and our people should be well housed enough to survive and thrive.
- Our world and our people should be well protected (exposures, crime) enough to survive and thrive.
- Our world and our people should be well educated enough to survive and thrive.
- Our world and our people should be physically and mentally well enough to survive and thrive.
- Our world and our people should be personally growing/developing well enough to survive and thrive.
- Our world should be good habitat enough to survive and thrive.
- Our world and our people should not be vulnerable.
- Our world and our people should be producing personal and public goods enough to survive and thrive.
- Our world should have a stable, positive climate.
- Our world and our people should be sustained.

Based on these overarching changes, use Table 7.4 to describe more specifically what all that has to change to progress from our world's current status to achieve our desired surviving and thriving status.

d. What actions are needed to achieve its thriving future? What actions are needed to bring about the needed changes (identified in "c") that improve our world's current status enough to achieve the desired surviving and thriving status? [Figure 7.1] [42]

Being well-off (financially). Being well nourished (food and drink).
Being well housed. Being well protected (exposures, crime). Being
well educated. Being physically and mentally well. Personally
growing/developing well. Living within good habitat. Not being
vulnerable. Producing personal and public goods. Living within a
stable, positive climate. Being sustained.

We identify actions that support <u>good</u> changes that will help improve
and/or sustain surviving and thriving. If good changes are likely to
occur, together we support them. If good changes are not likely to
occur, together we support them and develop other good changes to
compensate.

Use Table 7.4 to describe all the actions to be taken.

We identify actions that stop <u>bad</u> changes that prevent or limit
surviving and thriving. If bad changes are not likely to occur,
together we ensure they do not. If bad changes are likely to occur,
together we change them, stop them or avoid/reduce their impact.
As individual people, private business, interest groups/organizations,
countries and international organizations, together we should support
our jointly developed strategy and successfully take the actions to
ensure our world and each person in our world are performing well.

Overall *Thrive!* strategy and actions. Our overall *Thrive!* strategy
and actions need to be documented and agreed to by all of us - our
world's people and leaders. This will be our world's ***Thrive!***
Strategy and Action Plan.

---

[42] An action is defined as "who will do what to/with whom, where, when, and with
what result."

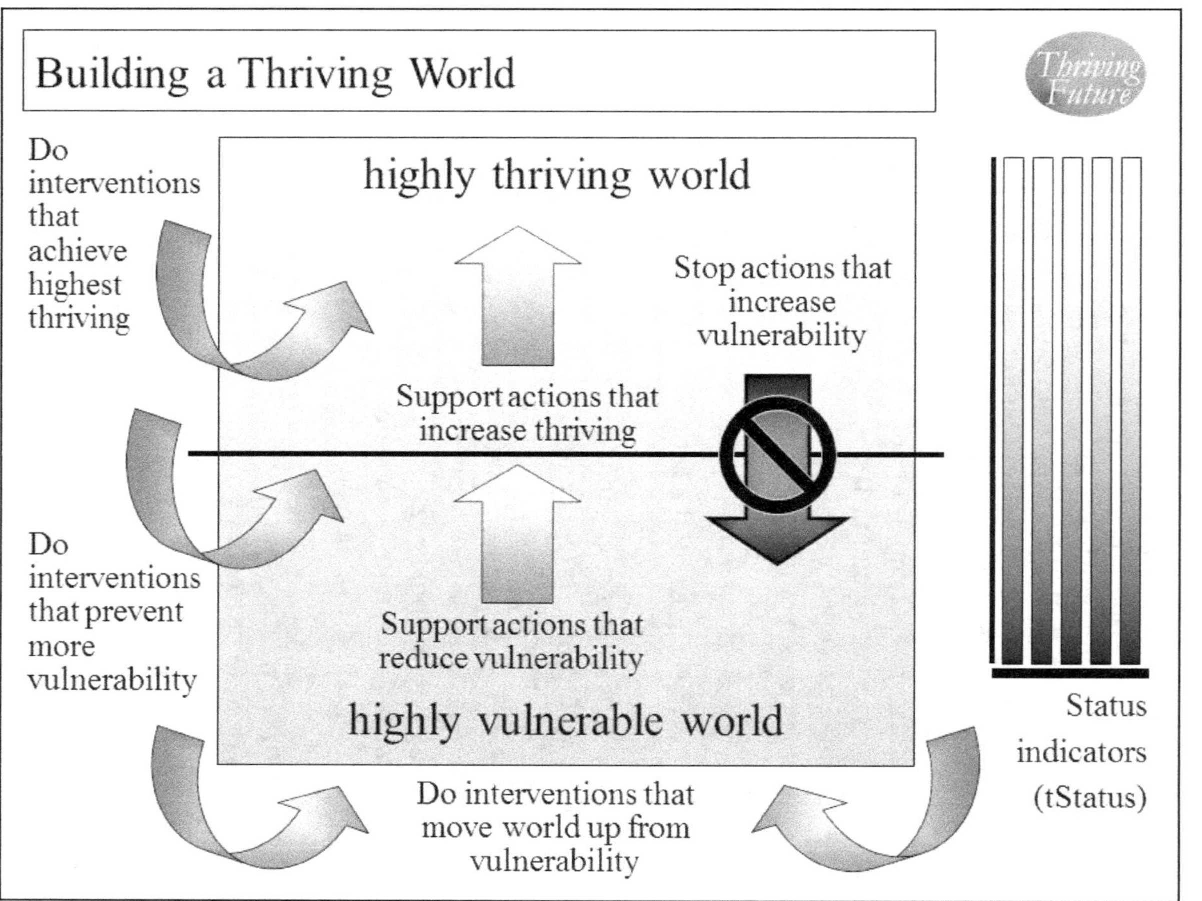

Figure 7.1. Building a Thriving World.

Different individual people, interest groups/organizations, countries and international organizations will take on different responsibilities. For each action, we designate who will do what to/with whom, where, when, and with what result. Use Table 7.4 to document these actions and responsibilities. We make sure we have all the actions that are needed to build, achieve and sustain our surviving and thriving world.

As the strategy is executed, our strategy, actions and results should be updated in our ***Thrive!* Strategy and Action Plan**.

Periodically, we should do an evaluation that assesses our world's strategies/actions near and long term impact on near and long term surviving and thriving. When a) our world's strategies and actions are not building and sustaining a thriving future and/or b) there are changes in our world, we should adjust our overall *Thrive!* strategy and actions.

The key is to successfully execute our world's ***Thrive!* Strategy and Action Plan** and to build a near and long term surviving and thriving future.[43] *[Following is an example of a stronger **Thrive! Strategy and Action Plan** for our world's surviving <u>and</u> thriving future.]*

---

[43] At this point, we have good information to execute our world's ***Thrive!*** Strategy and Action Plan. We can make progress. But, if feasible, we should develop our strategy and actions further using more of the tools and models already mentioned. This is very highly encouraged and is necessary because of our very, very complex world.

　As stated earlier, this "how-to", by design, is simple but powerful. It is relatively basic providing the framework for doing "our world" strategy. The optimal approach is to use this how-to framework <u>and</u> use the more extensive strategy, models and tools in a) the ***Thrive!* Next Generation Toolkit** contained in the full **People's Guide** and b) ***Thrive! - Building a Thriving Future*** available via <u>www.Amazon.com</u> or free download from <u>www.ThrivingFuture.org</u>.

Example of our world surviving <u>and</u> thriving. *To build, achieve and sustain a surviving <u>and</u> thriving future, the* **Thrive! Strategy and Action Plan** *for our world should be more like the following example: [Who will do what to/with whom, where, when, and with what result?]*

Starting immediately, we (people, business/industry, private organizations (local, country), governments (local, country) and international organizations) build, achieve, and sustain a surviving and thriving future for our world and for all forever, including:

- Performing well. *Starting immediately, people, business/industry, private organizations (local, country), governments (local, country) and international organizations act to ensure, within the next 20 years, a) all (who are able and not appropriately retired) can work and earn a living income sufficient to survive and thrive and b) all have sufficient resources for and are living, recreating, learning so that they are surviving and thriving to maximum extent feasible.*

- Being well-off (financially). *Starting immediately, people, business/industry, private organizations (local, country), governments (local, country) and international organizations act to ensure, within the next 20 years, a) all have sufficient income/resources to survive and thrive and b) all governments have sufficient resources to provide needed (supporting surviving) and desired (supporting thriving) public programs and policies.*

- Being well nourished (food and drink). *Starting immediately, people, business/industry, private organizations (local, country), governments (local, country) and international organizations act to ensure, within the next 20 years, that all people have access to, be able to afford and consume healthy foods enough to survive and thrive.*

- Being well housed. *Starting immediately, people, business/industry, private organizations (local, country), governments (local, country) and international organizations act to ensure, within the next 20 years, all have access to, be able to afford and live in adequate and preferably high performing housing that supports surviving and thriving.*

- Being well protected (exposures, crime). *Starting immediately, people, business/industry, private organizations (local, country), governments (local, country) and international organizations act to ensure, within the next 20 years, a) environmental exposures in home, workplace and elsewhere are minimized so as to not prevent surviving and thriving and b) crimes are minimized to the extent feasible in terms of frequency and impact so as to not prevent surviving and thriving.*

- Being well educated. *Starting immediately, people, business/industry, private organizations (local, country), governments (local, country) and international organizations act to ensure, within the next 20 years, all people are educated to the full extent of their abilities, needs and desires and to support their surviving and thriving.*

- Being physically and mentally well. *Starting immediately, people, business/industry, private organizations (local, country), governments (local, country) and international organizations act to ensure, within the next 20 years, a) all people receive the optimal health support to ensure, within the next 20 years, surviving and thriving and b) all people's physical and mental health is optimized to best ensure surviving and thriving.*

- Personally growing/developing well. *Starting immediately, people, business/industry, private organizations (local, country), governments (local, country) and international organizations act to ensure, within the next 20 years, all people are personally growing and developing to best ensure surviving and thriving.*

- Living within good habitat. *Starting immediately, people, business/industry, private organizations (local, country), governments (local, country) and international organizations act to ensure, within the next 20 years, a) all people have access to habitat that best supports their surviving and thriving and b) our world has the optimal mix, quantity and quality of habitat to best support our world and its inhabitants' surviving and thriving.*

- Not being vulnerable. *Starting immediately, people, business/industry, private organizations (local, country), governments (local, country) and international organizations act to ensure, within the next 20 years, our world and all of its people, if vulnerable, are vulnerable only to the minimum extent feasible.*

- Producing personal and public goods. *Starting immediately, people, business/industry, private organizations (local, country), governments (local, country) and international organizations act to ensure, within the next 20 years, our people produce personal and public goods (including personal income/resources, housing, food and drink, energy, education, health, protection, personal growth and development, and habitat) so as to support surviving and thriving for all persons and for our world overall.*

- Living within a stable, positive climate. *Starting immediately, people, business/industry, private organizations (local, country), governments (local, country) and international organizations act to ensure, within the next 10 years, all people behave so as to avoid negative impacts and support positive impacts so as to help ensure a stable, positive climate.*

- Being sustained. *Starting immediately, people, business/industry, private organizations (local, country), governments (local, country) and international organizations act to ensure, within the next 5 years, all people behave so as to ensure the sustainability of our world* <u>*and*</u> *its people.*

Chapter 8: Thrive! System© (TS). Achieve thriving people and communities with highest levels of thriving for all everywhere.

How Thrive! Systems help builds, achieves and sustains <u>a thriving future</u> <u>for people and communities.</u>

In the 1970s, inner city Milwaukee (WI) suffered from a severe shortage of health and related support for its low- and middle-income people. The author, serving as Director of Special Projects for the Milwaukee Health Department, designed and implemented a four-site personal support system providing support to inner city people. It was a rudimentary first instance of a Thrive! System. Bringing together a wide range of public and private organizations, a wide range of personal support was provided together in several sites. They included preventive health, public health, medical care, dental care, mental health care, social services, and financial assistance. This personal support was coordinated for persons by Nurse Coordinators in each site. The community was actively involved and supportive. The system was funded through a collaboration of the City, County, private hospitals, the dental school, The Robert Wood Johnson Foundation, Community Development Funds and waiver from the Medicare and Medicaid programs. This effort operated successfully for decades. While far short of what is described here as a Thrive! System, this effort served as a foundation for Thrive! Systems proposed here.

In previous chapters, vision and strategy for achieving thriving people and communities has been laid out. Also laid out has been the rationale for **Thrive! Systems (TS),** ideal systems that can help achieve that vision.

In our lives, if we survive birth, only two things are sure about our lives. We are born. We die. Everything else varies from person to person and over a person's lifetime.

Better than our current incomplete and inadequate personal support, a Thrive! System (TS) gives us our best chance to survive and thrive throughout our lifetime.[44] Our having a TS for our community ensures we are more thriving people in a more thriving community. (Table 8.1. Thrive! System – Helping Ensure Thriving for All)

A TS has persons and their communities at the center-. At the center with persons are their Primary Personal Support (PPS) surrounded by all needed and wanted Personal Support (PS). A TS adjusts when locations, time, person, and community change. It takes into account all of personal and community characteristics and all of health and well-being. It understands personal and community environment and its impact on thriving. It understands and uses the full range of thriving support to improve and sustain thriving. It connects all of these, with information and other support, into a fully integrated and supportive system for persons and their communities. (Figure 8.1. Thrive! Systems Ensure More Thriving People)

---

[44] Thrive! Systems (TS) are comprehensive systems that can be of almost any size and for any type of community. Community includes legal communities (e.g., village, town, city, county, State, nation), geographic areas (e.g., regions), groups (e.g. families, ethnic groups, affinity groups), and worlds.

Thrive! System – Helping Ensure Thriving For All [1]		
Vision		Thriving people and communities with highest levels of thriving for all everywhere.
Mission		Achieve thriving people and communities with highest levels of thriving for all everywhere.
System		<ul><li>Ensures accessible, affordable and high quality Personal Support for everyone in community.</li><li>Supports whole person and whole community's thriving rather than disconnected or partially connected support or supporting only parts of a person (e.g. only health) and a community.</li><li>Operates in partnership with the person and their family and community.</li><li>Provides a person-centered Primary Personal Support as the primary partner with the person to access and coordinate all needed Personal Support to achieve highest levels of thriving.</li><li>Provides a personal support system for persons and their Primary Personal Support.</li><li>Provides directly or indirectly the full range of Personal Support.</li><li>Provides directly and provides collaboratively via affiliations the full range of Personal Support to ensure accessibility for the person and the community.</li><li>Utilizes all payers (public, private and person) and optimizes costs to ensure affordability of Primary Personal Support and Personal Support for the person and the community.</li><li>Utilizes effective quality assurance collaboratively by Thrive! Systems and affiliated organizations to ensure high quality Primary Personal Support and Personal Support.</li><li>Ensures that all people, other creatures and Earth survive and thrive to maximum extent feasible.</li></ul>

[1] Thrive! System is the updated, upgraded and more comprehensive and complete version of system created for and implemented in inner city Milwaukee (WI) in late 1970s and which operated successfully for decades.

Table 8.1. Thrive! System – Helping Ensure Thriving for All.

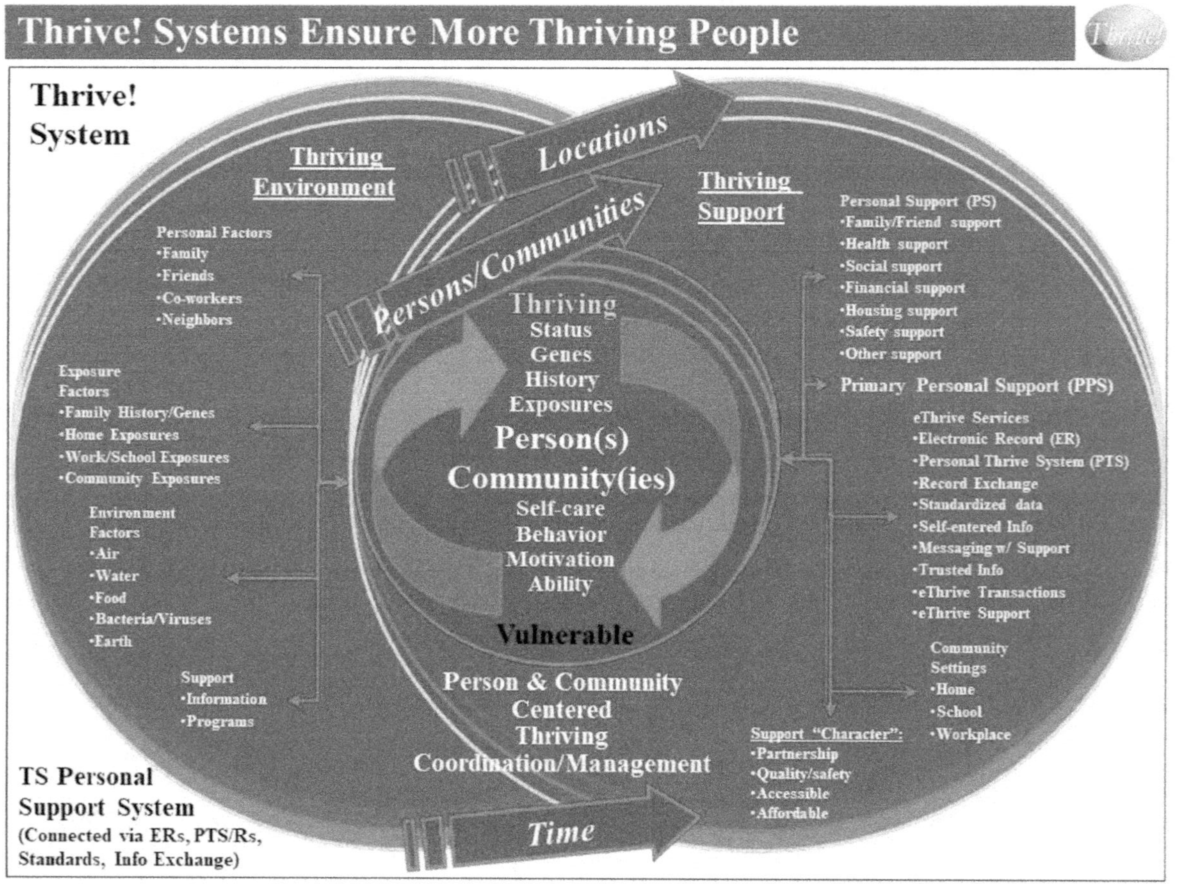

Figure 8.1. Thrive! Systems Ensure More Thriving People.

Thrive!

We want to thrive as much as possible over our lifetime.

We are born. If we live long enough, we are a child, an adult, and an older adult. Then we die. Over our lifetime and depending on how long we live, we may go through early development, may learn, may work, may expand our family, and may have post-work time. Then we die.

If we are fortunate, we live many years through all of these stages until we die a quick and painless death. If we are truly fortunate, we thrive through all of these stages. Very few of us will be that fortunate under the current incomplete and inadequate system.

During our lives after we are born, we may thrive and/or we may be vulnerable. Then we die.

We should want to thrive for as much of our lives as possible. We should do everything reasonable and possible to thrive. While we may be able and willing to do much by ourselves, we will be more successful with truly good partners (Primary Personal Support (PPS)) with all needed and wanted Personal Support (PS) in a truly good system (a Thrive! System (TS)). (Figure 8.2. Persons & Our Lifetime.)

What does it mean for us to thrive?

Very simply, we thrive when we do well throughout our lives. When our families and friends do well throughout their lives. When our communities do well now and for the long term. When our world does well now and for the long term.

More specifically, we, our families and friends, our communities and our world thrive when we are:
- Performing well,
- Well-off (financially),
- Well nourished,
- Well housed,
- Well protected (exposures, crime),
- Well educated,
- Physically and mentally well (people),
- Growing/developing well,
- Living within good habitat,

Thrive!

- Physically well (Earth, plants, animals, environment),
- Not vulnerable,
- Producing personal and public goods,
- Living within a stable, positive climate, and
- Sustained.

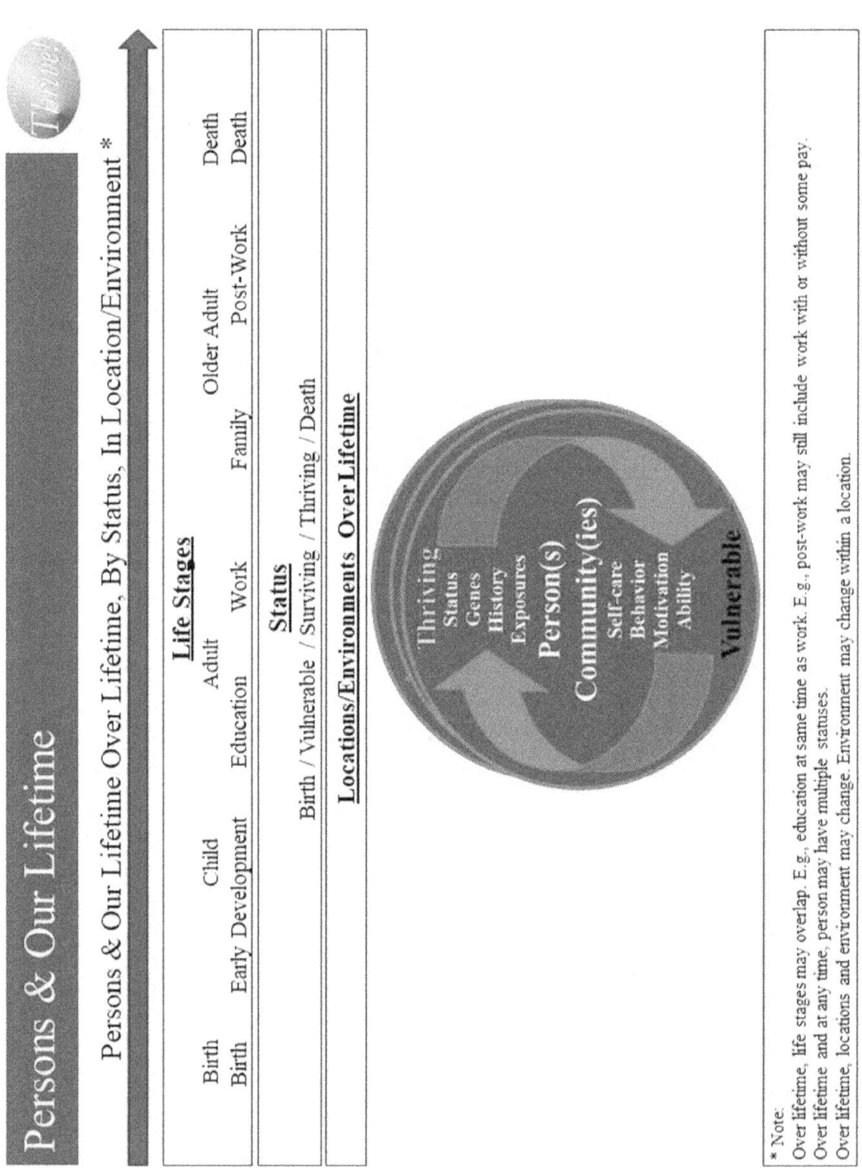

Figure 8.2. Persons & Our Lifetime.

We are more likely to thrive in a Thrive! System© (TS).

The U.S. Institute of Medicine (IOM) [now the National Academy of Medicine] provides a way of viewing a health system's performance through our eyes. What we want from a health system is that we are "staying healthy", "getting better", "living with illness or disability" and/or "coping with the end of life." Only considering health, this is a health system we want and need. This health system, a Thriving Health System, is described in **HealthePeople® - Achieving Health People, Communities & World Via Thrive!®**.

Going beyond health and taking this one more major positive step via a Thrive! System (TS), we "start and stay thriving", "get better (from vulnerable to thriving) faster", "live as well as possible with illness or disability" and/or "cope as well as possible with end of life." Some of us may experience more than one of these at the same time. IOM's quality reports have six aims for a high performing health system. They stress it should be safe, effective, person/patient-centered, timely, efficient, and equitable. Going further, a Thrive! System should be safe, effective, person- and community-centered, efficient and equitable, and should help achieve thriving for both a person and a community.

Building on and going beyond the IOM work, a TS should perform well from the person's perspective and a community's perspective. As depicted in the attached figure, a TS would "check all the boxes." (Figure 8.3. Thrive! System's Six Aims & Person's and Community's Perspective on Thriving) As suggested earlier, a TS can, should and will do much better.

To get to the personal support we truly want and need, we need a TS that has us and our Primary Personal Support (PPS) at the center. Together as partners from birth to death, we access whatever other support is needed to help us start and stay thriving, help us get better (from vulnerable to thriving) faster, help us live as well as possible with illness or disability, and help us cope as well as possible with end of life.

Six Aims & Person/Community's Perspective on Thriving

Supportive of Institute of Medicine principles and aims. a Thrive! System supports persons, communities and their Primary Personal Support, and the rest of Personal Support in continuing to innovate and find better ways to achieve thriving.

Aims for Personal Support Performance/Quality. Achieve Thriving for Both Person and Community.

Person & Community's Perspective on Needs	Safe	Effective	Person & Community centered	Timely	Efficient	Equitable
Start & stay thriving	+	+	+	+	+	+
Get better (from vulnerable to thriving) faster	+	+	+	+	+	+
Live as well as possible with illness or disability	+	+	+	+	+	+
Cope as well as possible with end of life	+	+	+	+	+	+

Figure 8.3. Six Aims & Person's and Community's Perspective on Thriving.

Can we transform what we have into TS? Yes, but not easily. Most of the elements exist in our current communities. But they are poorly organized, poorly connected and poorly communicating. The first step is to put in place the Primary Personal Supports (PPS) and connect them to us and the

Thrive!

rest of Personal Support (PS). We need to improve and organize the existing PS elements so they better provide and coordinate personal support. We need a lifetime electronic personal support system that tracks and appropriately shares both our interactions with our PPS and all other PS and appropriately and carefully tracks our own personal needs, wants, behaviors and conditions. We need our PPS and ourselves to appropriately share our information carefully and accurately only with whom we want when we want and how we want.

We are more likely to thrive in a Thrive! System© (TS) that addresses the whole person and the whole community.

A Thrive! System (TS) is very different from what we have today. TS addresses the whole person, not just piecemeal parts of the person. TS addresses the whole community, not just piecemeal parts of the community.

What we have today is a piecemeal approach to persons. It is more problem by problem oriented than effectively dealing with the <u>full range</u> of problems experienced by persons at a point in time or over their lifetime. Health is generally addressed separately from housing. Housing from income. Work from school. Public safety from environmental protection. Etc. The same is generally true for a community.

What we have today is more oriented toward solving individual problems rather than being oriented toward solving <u>all</u> problems that a person experiences. The same is generally true for a community.

What we have today is more oriented toward solving problems than <u>helping the whole person thrive</u>. The same is generally true for a community

What we have today is a non-system in which different parts of personal support are poorly coordinated, are disconnected and communicate poorly.

What we have today is a non-system where persons are essentially on their own when it comes to addressing the whole set of factors that reduce vulnerability and increase thriving. Not only is the person not well served but the community is not well served.

Very differently and much more effectively, a TS has a PPS for each person who partners with the person to address all factors that reduce vulnerability and increase thriving.

Very differently and much more effectively, a TS is fully coordinated, is fully connected and communicates well among persons, their Primary Personal Support (PPS), and their total Personal Support (PS). A TS addresses all the factors in a person's life that reduce vulnerability and increase thriving. A TS addresses all the factors in a community that reduce vulnerability and increase thriving.

We are more likely to thrive with a Primary Personal Support (PPS) partner in a Thrive! System© (TS).
A Primary Personal Support (PPS) functions as a partner with us within our community. A partner who brings more knowledge about how to reduce vulnerability and increase thriving than we have and who supports our efforts to thrive. This partner would preferably be a person with specific training and experience to be a PPS. This partner must be well trained and may come from a range of professions, including a social worker or a nurse.

On our behalf, a PPS partners with the rest of Primary Support (PS) across as many life stages and as much of our life as is appropriate and feasible.

Our PPS partner knows us, knows our key thriving and vulnerability factors, knows our needs and wants, knows our behaviors, knows our living and work environment, and provides continuity over as much of our lifetime as possible. Our PPS partner helps us start and stay thriving, helps us get better (from vulnerable to thriving) faster, helps us live as well as possible with illness or disability, and helps us cope as well as possible with end of life. (Figure 8.4. Persons & Our Personal Support)

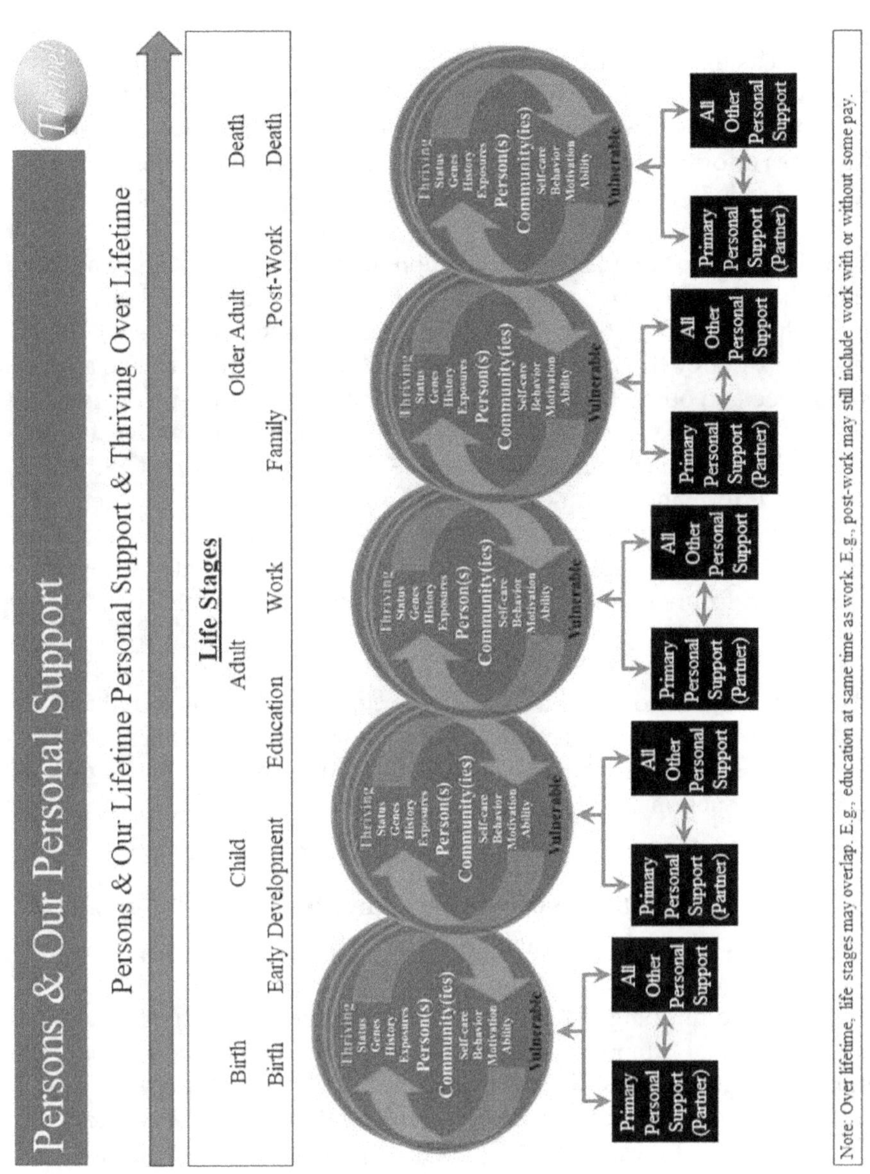

Figure 8.4. Persons & Our Personal Support.

We are more likely to thrive by having and using Thrive! System© (TS) personal support systems for persons and their Primary Personal Support (PPS). [45]

---

[45] The TS personal support system is also known as a "Thrive! System", a

As is increasingly the case with respect to health, persons and their Primary Personal Support (PPS) need personal support systems to help them collect and store personal information, access electronic support resources (information and tools), and decide and adjust the best path and actions to reduce vulnerability and increase thriving.

These Thrive! System (TS) personal support systems collect and hold the personal information on persons that relate to vulnerability and thriving. They help persons and their PPS assess the current status and develop and adjust the strategy that will achieve the most thriving. They utilize artificial intelligence and other decision support mechanisms to support decision-making. They track progress toward reducing vulnerability and increasing thriving. They help connect to and use the full range of internet and other electronic information and personal support resources. They enable communication and information sharing between persons and their PPS and with any other needed Personal Support (PS). They enable information to be moved from one PPS to a subsequent PPS. They enable connecting information on and for members of a family.

When persons want or need information or to take an action to reduce vulnerability or increase thriving, the TS personal support systems enable them to get the information, make better decisions, and effectively take the best action or actions.

We are more likely to thrive by using all needed Personal Support (PS) partners in a Thrive! System© (TS).

To address the full range of conditions we may face in our lives, our Primary Personal Support (PPS) and we both need all needed Personal Support (PS) as partners. We need partners to help successfully address conditions such as an acute illness or injury, a chronic illness and/or a disability. Each of these conditions often require additional skills and knowledge. Maybe a specialist or subspecialist. Maybe rehabilitation people. Maybe a therapist of one kind or another. Maybe home care or community care people. Maybe a palliative or hospice care team.

---

subsystem of the overall TS.

PS may include family and friends. It may include public social services and financial assistance. May include spiritual healers, public health, and personal assistants. May include schools and employers. May include public safety people. May include food and nutrition people.

PS may be any one of the full range of personal support that can and should be provided when needed. Many different types of people and organizations will have the skills and knowledge to be partners and help address conditions. Depending on our need, any of these people may have an important role as partners in helping us start and stay thriving, helping us get better (from vulnerable to thriving) faster, helping us live as well as possible with illness or disability, and helping us cope as well as possible with end of life.

Our having full "Personal Support (PS)" is more and better than what supports us today.

To keep ourselves thriving, traditional personal support is not enough. While traditional support has a very important role to play, we need more and better support. Full Personal Support (PS) is more complete and is the full range of people, goods and services that can help us thrive as much as possible. This includes the partners described above. But it also includes electronic support (e.g. internet information, apps and devices, messaging, our personal record) and devices, sensors, computers, smartphones, tablets and many more support tools yet to come. A Thrive! System (TS) has the types of personal support we have today plus other important personal support and plus future personal support yet to be available or even developed.

At the center of a TS are persons and their Primary Personal Support (PPS). Together, they access whatever PS is wanted or needed. Traditional PS services may include health care and social services. When needed for a severe or terminal illness, PS may also include hospice and palliative care. When a person has a disability, PS may include personal assistance or home care. When a person has multiple issues, the Primary Personal Support (PPS) is especially important.

In the following figure, many more of the potential PS are detailed. But even this is not a complete PS list. (Figure 8.5. Thrive! Systems – Person and Primary and Other Personal Support.)

- Support For Thriving
- Support Against Vulnerability
- Community Support
- Family/Friends Support
- Financial/Income Support
- Health Support
- Food/Nutrition Support
- Disability Support
- End of Life Support
- Education/Training Support
- Supportive Environment/Habitat
- Housing Support
- Internet Info & Services
- Protection from Crime
- Protection from Exposures
- Growth & Development Support

There are many other types of personal support that are part of a TS. There is information that is provided through understanding a person's history, family history, environmental history, education history, work history and genetic makeup.

There is also indirect support, support that may never touch the person directly but that helps reduce vulnerability and increase thriving for the person. Examples of indirect support include advocacy, government executive and legislative branches, environmental protection, workplace protection, health-related research, food production, regulation, and standards setting.

In a TS, personal support is whatever support a person wants and needs that will improve or maintain thriving or will help a person who is vulnerable with a disability and/or with a terminal illness or injury. The PPS partners with a person to make best use of any or all available personal support.

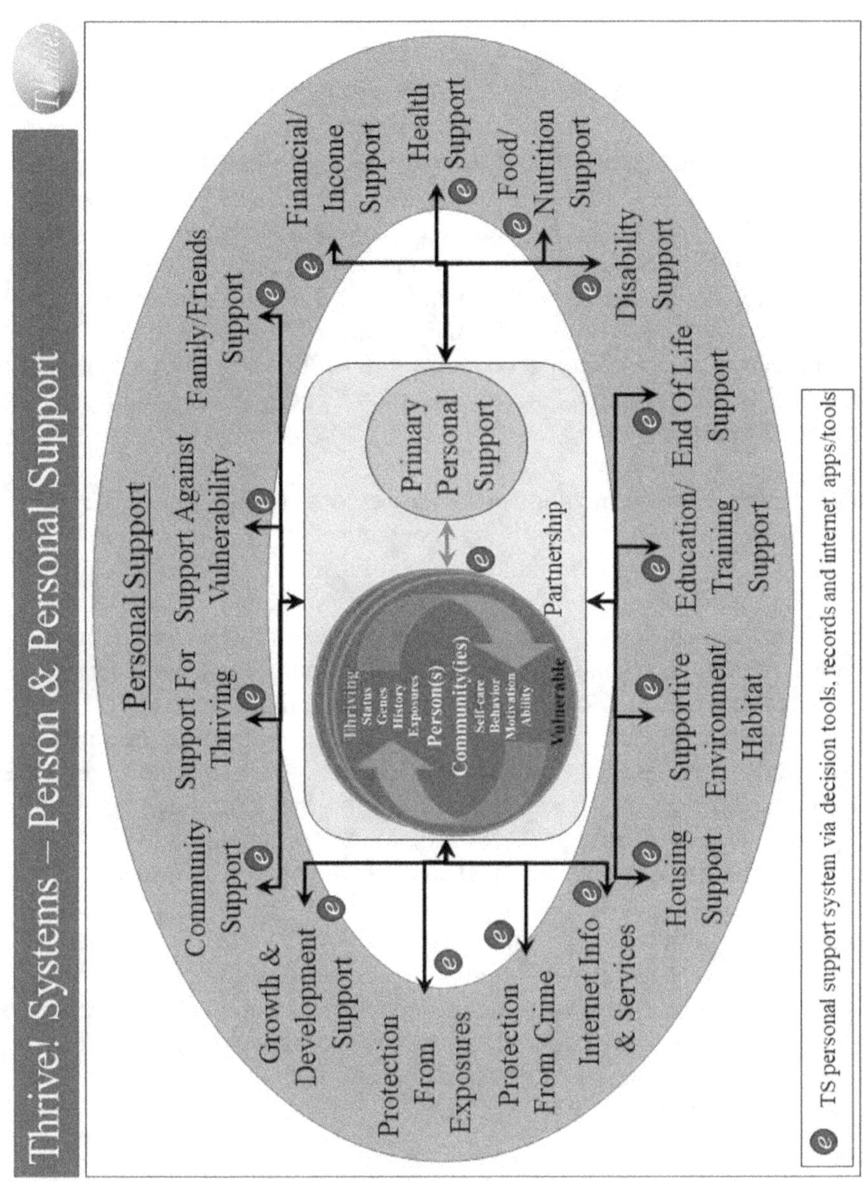

Figure 8.5. Thrive! Systems – Person and Primary and Other Personal Support.

Together in a TS, all of this personal support best supports persons and their PPS as they partner to help start and stay thriving, get better (from vulnerable to thriving) faster, live as well as possible with illness or disability, and cope as well as possible with end of life.

How is a Thrive! System© (TS) best organized to help us?

A Thrive! System (TS) for a community may provide personal support via a fully integrated TS (single organization with Primary Personal Support (PPS) at the center) and/or partially-integrated TS (well-connected multiple organizations with one or more Primary Personal Support at one or more centers). They both can support persons, their PPS and all other Personal Support (PS). (Figure 8.6. Thrive! Systems – Person & Community Centered Organizations.)

Public and private organizations provide personal support that is key to maintaining and improving thriving. Together, they should include PPS and other Personal Support, including health care, skilled nursing home, long term nursing home, home care, personal assistance, rehabilitation, illness/injury specific support, public health, nutrition, emotional support, hospice, palliative, and holistic therapies. They should include social service, food/nutrition, housing, income support, financial services, payment for health care, personal security, justice, education/training, environmental protection, regulation, roads, parks, waste disposal, utilities, libraries, and emergency assistance. Some employers provide personal support in- and/or outside of the workplace. Some schools provide personal support. The Federal government provides national security.

Connecting all of this PS with persons and their PPS are TS personal support systems that can and should hold and process information to be shared carefully and only when needed, appropriate and authorized. They must be able to exchange information in a standardized way that supports effective decision-making for the person, for a person's PPS and for a person and community's PS.

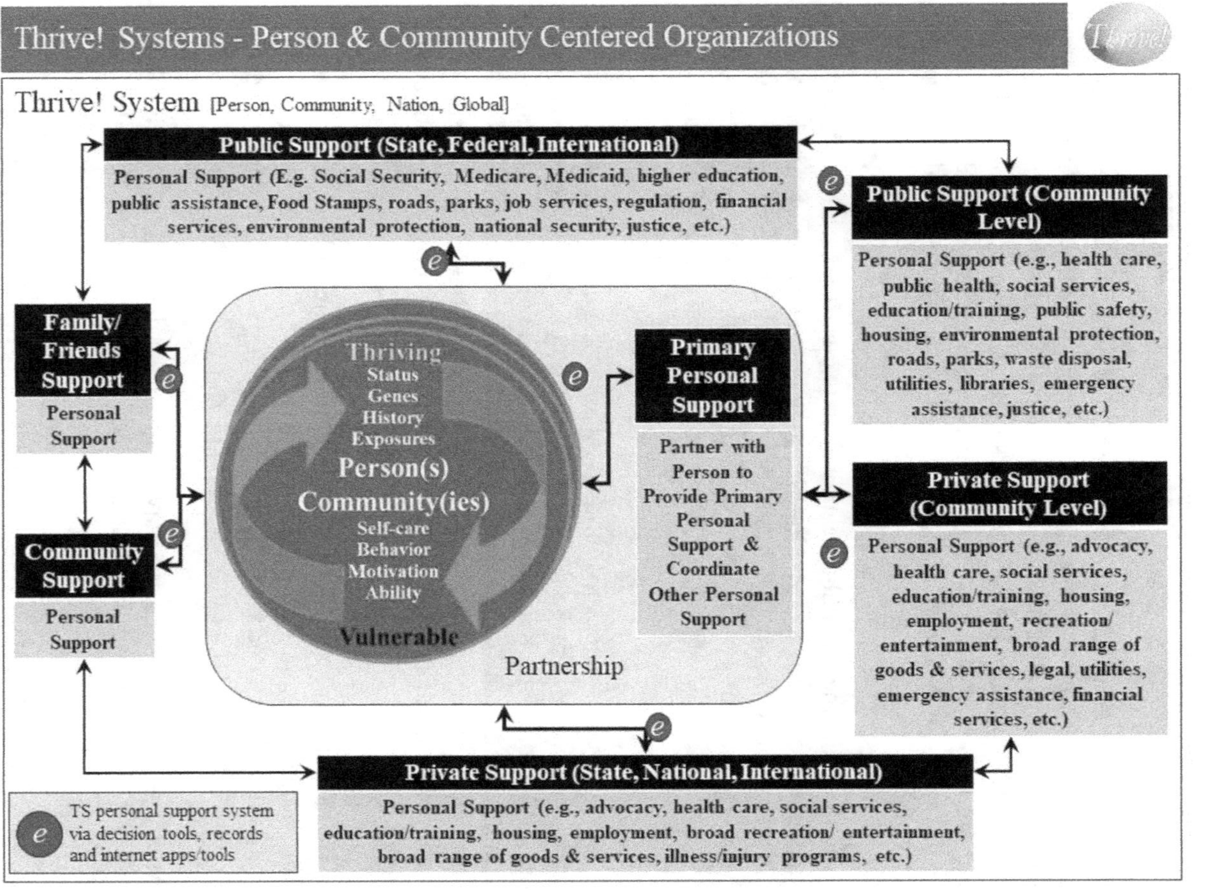

Figure 8.6. Thrive! Systems - Person & Community Centered Organizations.

Thrive!

How does a Thrive! System© (TS) support a person and a community?

A Thrive! System (TS) supports a person or persons from beginning to end. Prior to birth, we, via our family, are partnered with a Primary Personal Support (PPS). Starting with our birth and through childhood, we have a PPS partner. The PPS partners with us as individuals or with us and our family and helps us access all other Personal Support (PS). As children and as we grow, we take an increasing part in our own pursuit of thriving. The more the better.

When we become an adult, we may change our PPS partner. Our respective roles are similar. Our PPS may be one with more skills and knowledge to support our adult lives. As an adult and to the extent we can, we take on a stronger role in our pursuit of thriving. The more the better. If we have a family, we and our family may partner with a PPS as a family unit.

In our later years when any children have moved on to their own lives and we may experience more illness or disabling conditions, we may change our PPS to one who has more skills and knowledge with illness and/or disabling conditions. We and our PPS will need to access the PS that can best help us manage illnesses or disabling conditions. To the extent we are able, we should take a strong role in our pursuit of thriving. The more the better.

If we have a terminal illness or are just nearing the end of our lives as part of normal aging, our PPS may be one who can best help us best cope with end of life. We should live this part of our lives as independently and with as much dignity and quality of life as possible. The more the better.

At any point in our lives, we may experience a major illness or disabling condition that requires us to partner with a PPS with that skill and knowledge.

In a TS, all wanted and needed PS must be physically accessible. This is particularly challenging in rural areas but more doable today with internet and other communication resources. Special provisions must be made for people with physical or cognitive limitations.

Even if all this PS is available, interconnected and accessible, financial access must be ensured. PS must be affordable for all payers, including the person. Today, this is through private support, public support, charity and self-pay. There are possibly better ways a TS can ensure financial access. In a TS, no person fails to receive wanted and needed PS due to financial limitations or inability.

What will our lives be like in a Thrive! System© (TS)?

Starting with our birth and through childhood, we and our families and our Primary Personal Support (PPS) focus on how to increase and sustain thriving in the way we live our daily lives. Eat and drink healthier. Exercise better. Avoid or minimize environmental risks. Get age-appropriate health and well-being exams. Treat illnesses and injuries early and well. Obtain education and training. Track our personal vulnerability and thriving. Use effective Personal Support (PS) partners. Take responsibility for our and our family's thriving and for our community's thriving. Together, these actions help us reduce vulnerability and increase thriving.

When we become an adult, we take more responsibility for our own vulnerability and thriving. But we still do so in partnership with our PPS. We continue to eat and drink healthier. Exercise better. Avoid or minimize environmental risks. Get age-appropriate health and well-being exams. Treat illnesses and injuries early and well. Continue to learn and develop. Ensure our food and housing. Ensure our financial viability now and through the end of our lives. Ensure our personal safety. Track our personal vulnerability and thriving. Learn more about our specific risks from family history, genetic make-up, environmental risks, and how we live our lives. Together, these actions help us reduce vulnerability and increase thriving, help us deal with vulnerabilities earlier and better, and help us reduce vulnerability and increase thriving.

In our later years when any children have moved on to their own lives and we may experience more illness or disabling conditions, we continue with our PPS and with what we have been doing throughout our adulthood. But now we may be experiencing even more vulnerability, more illnesses, more disabling conditions, more of these at the same time and more severe versions of these. Together, we and our PPS help us reduce vulnerability, prevent illness and injury, help us deal with vulnerabilities earlier and better, help us reduce the severity of these, help us better deal with simultaneous vulnerabilities, help us better cope with a chronic or disabling condition, help us better deal with simultaneous and different PS, and help us reduce vulnerability and increase thriving.

If we have a terminal illness or are just nearing the end of our lives as part of normal aging, our PPS may be one who can best help us best cope with end of life. We still try to thrive as best we can given that we are nearing the end. Managing pain better. Prioritizing what PS are done or not done. Addressing emotional issues better for ourselves and our family and friends. Making sure we have our final arrangements in order. Handling the end of our lives as we want and with dignity.

Across and throughout our lives, we effectively use effective PS partners. We take responsibility for our and our family's health and well-being and for our community's health and well-being.

We want our "status" to improve from "worst thriving (highly vulnerable)" to "best thriving (highly thriving)" status. (Figure 8.7. Thriving Status – Move From Vulnerable To Thriving.)

It is worst when we are highly vulnerable and experience low personal and support ability, low personal and support motivation, unsupportive "environment", poor prevention outcomes, poor treatment and intervention outcomes, high risk for adverse events, high morbidity, low quality of life, high mortality, low life expectancy, and low satisfaction with PPS and PS.

It is best when we are highly thriving and experience high personal and support ability, high personal and support motivation, supportive "environment", good prevention outcomes, good treatment and intervention outcomes, low risk for adverse events, low morbidity, high quality of life, low mortality, high life expectancy, and high satisfaction with PPS and PS.

We need to move each element of our lives from being worst (highly vulnerable) to being best (highly thriving). Move to best outcomes and status. Move to thriving. We do that best in a Thrive! System (TS).

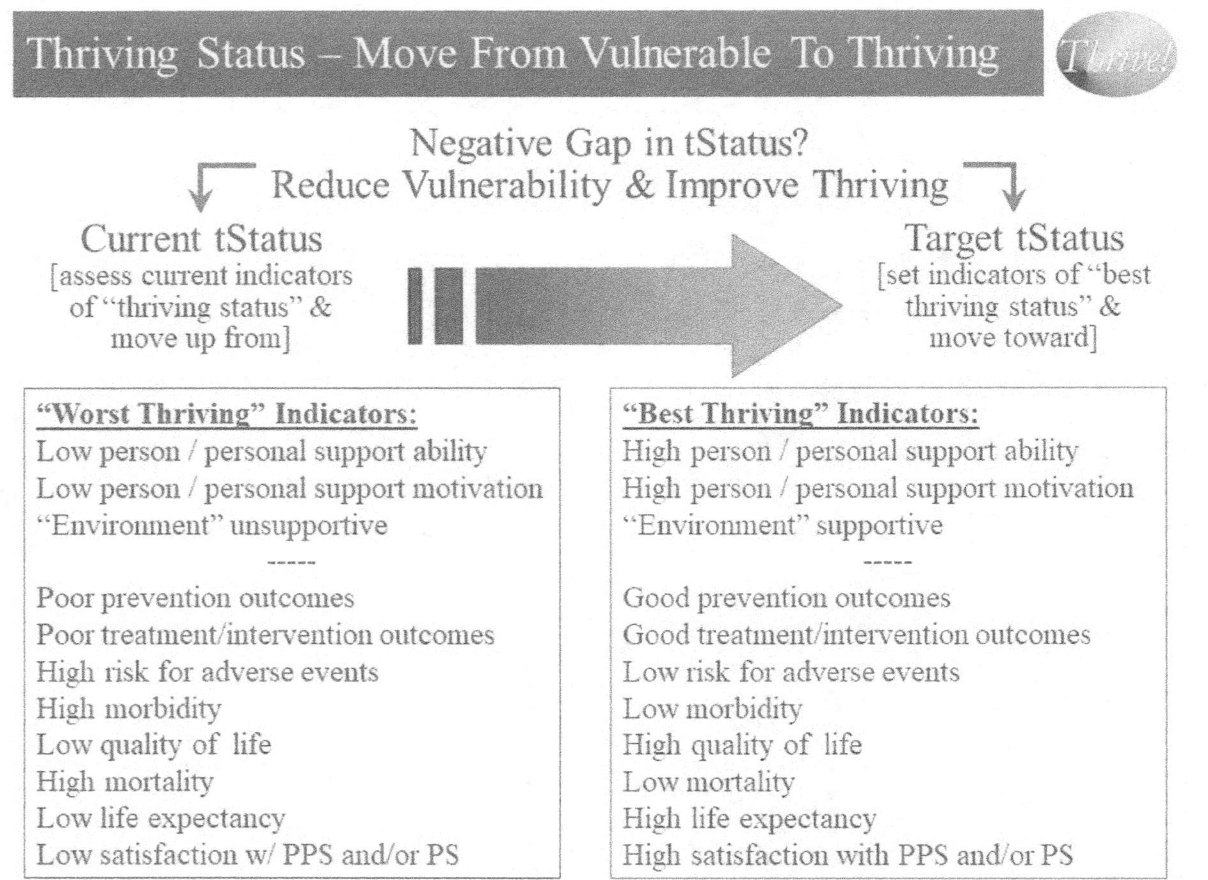

Figure 8.7. Thriving Status – Move From Vulnerable To Thriving.

How will we know when we are successful? When we are thriving? As noted earlier, thriving is when we are: performing well, well-off (financially), well nourished, well housed, well protected (exposures, crime), well educated, physically and mentally well (people), growing/developing well, living within good habitat, physically well (Earth, plants, animals, environment), not vulnerable, producing personal and public goods, living within a stable, positive climate, and sustained.

Our having Thrive! Systems© (TS) can and should achieve thriving people and communities for all everywhere.

Thrive!® and Thrive! Systems (TS) have a vision of thriving people and communities for all everywhere. They have the strategy to achieve that vision. (Figure 8.8. Thrive! Systems – Help Achieve Thriving).

The strategy is for us to thrive as best we can by doing the following:
- Stop actions that increase vulnerability.
- Support actions that increase thriving.
- Support actions that reduce vulnerability.
- Do interventions that best achieve highest thriving.
- Do interventions that best prevent more vulnerability.
- Do interventions that move up from vulnerability.

This is the Thrive!® vision for Thrive! Systems and for us and the communities these systems support.[46] As people, communities, nations and world, we should proceed toward the vision of achieving thriving people and communities for all everywhere.

---

[46] Thrive!® - Vision, mission, strategy and supportive tools help create and sustain large, positive and timely change and build a thriving future for all forever. They help build a thriving and surviving future:
- Vision: All thrive forever. All includes persons, communities, and world.
- Mission: Large, positive, timely change achieving surviving and thriving future for all forever.
- Strategy: A joint Thrive! Endeavor and call to action building a thriving future for all forever.

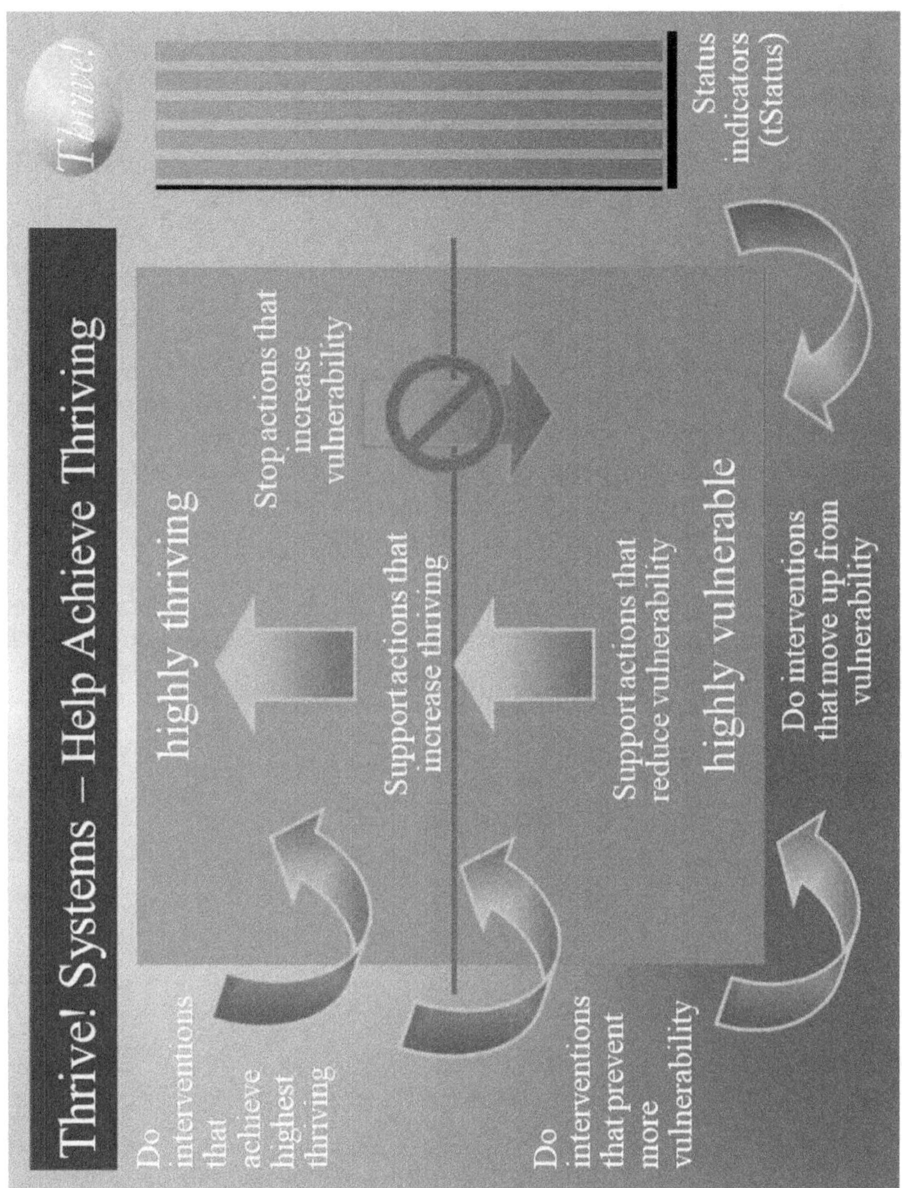

Figure 8.8. Thrive! Systems – Help Achieve Thriving.

We do this via a strategy of TS for all people and communities everywhere. TS are self-perpetuating, very affordable, easily accessible, "e" enabled, person-centered, prevention-oriented, and high quality systems. They produce high outcomes and status (thriving).

Such TS, partly physical and partly virtual and put into place by collaborative private and public partnerships, will greatly improve accessibility, quality and affordability for all people everywhere. They will greatly reduce vulnerability and increase thriving for all people everywhere and for all other creatures and for Earth.

Every community everywhere should have an effective and comprehensive TS. By every community having an effective and comprehensive TS, we can help people and communities thrive everywhere in the world. Every community's TS should effectively connect with every other community's TS. Together, they can best support people as they move amongst the world's communities. Together, they can share valuable resources to most efficiently and effectively support people and their communities. Together, they can best support people, their communities and the world, including the Earth upon which we depend for our continuing existence and thriving.

We can and should build and sustain TS for all people everywhere. We can and should achieve substantially more thriving people, communities, nations and world. We can and should move toward a truly thriving world. All people everywhere deserve and should expect nothing less.

Chapter 9: How the *Thrive!* Endeavor, you and all of us together, builds a thriving future.

How the *Thrive!* **Endeavor**, you and all of us together, builds, achieves and sustains <u>a thriving future</u> <u>for all</u> <u>forever</u>.

Thrive! Survive! Vulnerable! These are the keys to a call for creating and sustaining large, positive and timely change and building a surviving and thriving future. We are all vulnerable to some extent but that can change for the better. ***Thrive!*** is that call to action and a rallying cry for a better and thriving future. It is a vision and a mission for those wanting to build a better future. To achieve that vision and succeed with the mission, the ***Thrive!*** **Endeavor**, all of us together, strives to energize and empower people to build a thriving future for our families and friends, communities, countries and world. It strives to build, achieve and sustain a surviving and thriving future for all forever, to the maximum extent possible.[47] This future is ***Thrive!*** and is a bold vision and mission.

We have laid out why (Chapters 2 and 3) and how (Chapters 4 through 8) to build a surviving and thriving future for you and your family and friends, for you and your community, for you and your country, and for you and our world. But to truly have a thriving future, we need to have it for you and <u>everybody's</u> family and friends and <u>every</u> community and <u>every</u> country and <u>every part of</u> <u>and our entire</u> world. When all this comes together, you and all of us

---

[47] We must keep in mind that "our world" and "all" is expanding as we explore and move beyond earth to other parts of our universe. For that reason, "a thriving future for all forever" reaches as far as we reach or hope to reach.

will have built, achieved and sustained a surviving and thriving future.

How best to do this? We bring all this together with the *Thrive!* **Endeavor** where you and all of us together, build, achieve and sustain <u>a thriving future</u> <u>for all</u> <u>forever</u>. Creating and sustaining this vast human endeavor is the driving purpose and mission of this **Guide**.

Why the *Thrive!* Endeavor?

As laid out in Chapters 2 and 3, you and all of us want and need a surviving and thriving future because of our endangered future and our human need to survive and desire to thrive. And <u>only people</u> can and must fix all that is broken. And <u>only people</u> can and must build, achieve and sustain a survivable and thriving future. And <u>only all of us joined together</u> can succeed due to the scope (all), level (surviving and thriving), duration (forever) of the challenge. For these reasons, building, achieving and sustaining a surviving and thriving future requires a vast, sustained *Thrive!* **Endeavor** of all of us together.

What is the *Thrive!* Endeavor?

The *Thrive!* **Endeavor** is all of us together. It is vision, mission, strategy and call to action. Its vision is a surviving and thriving future for all forever. Its mission is to create and sustain large positive and timely change that builds, achieves and sustains a surviving and thriving future for all forever, to the maximum extent possible. Its strategy is to energize and empower all of us together in the vast, sustained human endeavor building and sustaining a thriving future. Its call for action is to motivate all of us (individual people, groups of people, private sector organizations, governments) to seek a thriving future, to create and sustain the necessary large positive change, and to work together to build, achieve and sustain a surviving and thriving future.

Thrive!

In support of this vision and mission, the Endeavor adopts and embraces "<u>A People's Constitution</u>" - "We the people, in order to form a more perfect union, commit to a thriving future for all forever." [48]

Who is and will be the *Thrive!* Endeavor?

The ***Thrive!* Endeavor** is <u>all of us together</u> building, achieving and sustaining a surviving and thriving future. "All of us together" include individual people, groups of people, private sector organizations and governments. "All of us together" include <u>current and future generations</u>. "All of us together" include <u>you</u>, and <u>everybody's</u> family and friends, and <u>every</u> community, and <u>every</u> country, and <u>every part of and our entire</u> world.

Who does what and how in the *Thrive!* Endeavor?

What the ***Thrive!* Endeavor** does and how it does it is different than past and current approaches which have major limitations and defects. The Endeavor is unique and better because it:
- Strives to achieve a thriving and sustainable future for all forever, to the maximum extent possible. But it also helps ensure survival, a necessary but not sufficient step to achieving a thriving future
- Enables the building of a surviving and thriving future for you, your family and friends, your community, your country and our world.
- Joins people of all backgrounds/generations together to achieve a thriving future.
- Is able to address every person, community and issue.
- Uses whole "community" (local, regional, state, country, world/global) strategy for creating and sustaining change and building thriving futures. [No longer should we rely on piecemeal strategies.]

---

[48] The **People's Constitution** should be just this brief, understandable and powerful. It should not replace any country's constitution. The intent is for it to be embraced by and acted upon affirmatively by all people forever.

- Uses whole "person" strategy for creating and sustaining change and building thriving futures. [No longer is the focus only on parts (ill health, hunger, poor education or insufficient income).]
- Uses whole "system" (community, health, education, economy, housing, etc.) strategy for creating and sustaining change and building thriving futures. [No longer should we rely on survival and piecemeal strategies for just parts of a system.]
- Takes an integrated approach to cross-cutting issues.
- Uses an integrated approach to people/environment strategy, change and thriving futures. [No longer is the focus only on people or the environment.]
- Uses a "person-centered" strategic approach that recognizes people's behaviors are the problem and the solution. [No longer should we fail to address "people's behavior".]
- Uses eMedia and social networking to expand communication and joint action and to activate and coordinate a large endeavor in "real time".
- Uses the *Thrive!* **Next Generation Toolkit** [in the full **People's Guide**] of strategy, models and tools to create and sustain change and build thriving futures. [No longer should we rely on past approaches that failed or had limited success.]
- Uses strategic/operational planning and combines it with strategic/operational execution.
- Creates a collaborative strategy with the necessary positive actions to build, achieve and sustain a surviving and thriving future.

To improve our chances of success, the ***Thrive!* Endeavor** recognizes and will positively use tipping points, a critical element in positive change efforts historically.[49] Throughout human history, we see moments when "tipping points" exist. Tipping points can enable negative or positive change. We see moments when a positive action is taken at a tipping point and major positive change occurs. We are now at such a tipping point. We are now at an historical moment when government and the private sector are broken in many ways, when our resources are becoming increasingly limited, when our environment is increasingly and negatively impacted, when our future is endangered, and when a failure to act positively dooms us to a failed, potentially non-survivable future. But, it is also a historical moment when we are the most able to change all that for the better. At this tipping point when our future is most endangered and we are most able, carefully developed and positive actions are more necessary and more likely to be effective and successful.

As laid out above in this Chapter and in Chapters 4 through 8, each and all of us should develop and take as many positive actions as we can. The more positive actions taken, the better for all of us. Each

---

[49] Using tipping points can be very helpful in building a thriving future. However, positive change efforts can also occur without an existing tipping point or without any tipping point. It is just more difficult. Where feasible, we should use current, future and creatable tipping points:
- Use current tipping points.
- Partner with families and friends, communities and countries that are broken and/or with clearly endangered futures.
- Partner with families and friends, communities and countries that are positioned to move up from surviving to thriving.
- Build off issue areas and cross-cutting issue areas that are broken and/or with endangered futures.
- Use breakthroughs in knowledge and technology.
- Partner with new, more capable and more motivated leaders emerge.
- Use eMedia and social networking.
- Use grassroots and self-organizing movements.
- Watch for and use new tipping points as they emerge.
- When necessary, appropriate and doable, create new tipping points that are opportunities to build a thriving future.

and all of us should help build, achieve and sustain a surviving and thriving future for <u>our family and friends</u>. Each and all of us should help build, achieve and sustain a surviving and thriving future for <u>our community</u>. Each and all of us should help build, achieve and sustain a surviving and thriving future for <u>our country</u>. Each and all of us should help build, achieve and sustain a surviving and thriving future for <u>our world</u>, including the Earth on which we depend. Via these actions and the *Thrive!* **Endeavor**, <u>each and all of us together</u> should build, achieve and sustain a surviving and thriving future.

What positive actions are needed to bring about the needed changes that improve our current status enough to achieve the desired surviving and thriving status? [Figure 9.1] Each and all of us identify actions that support <u>good</u> changes that will help reduce vulnerability and/or improve and/or sustain surviving and thriving. If good changes are likely to occur, together we support them. If good changes are not likely to occur, together we support them and develop other good changes to compensate.

Each and all of us identify actions that stop <u>bad</u> changes that increase vulnerability and/or prevent or limit surviving and thriving. If bad changes are not likely to occur, together we ensure they do not. If bad changes are likely to occur, together we change them, stop them or avoid/reduce their impact.

Via the Endeavor, all of us together develop our strategy and successfully take the actions to ensure a surviving and thriving future.

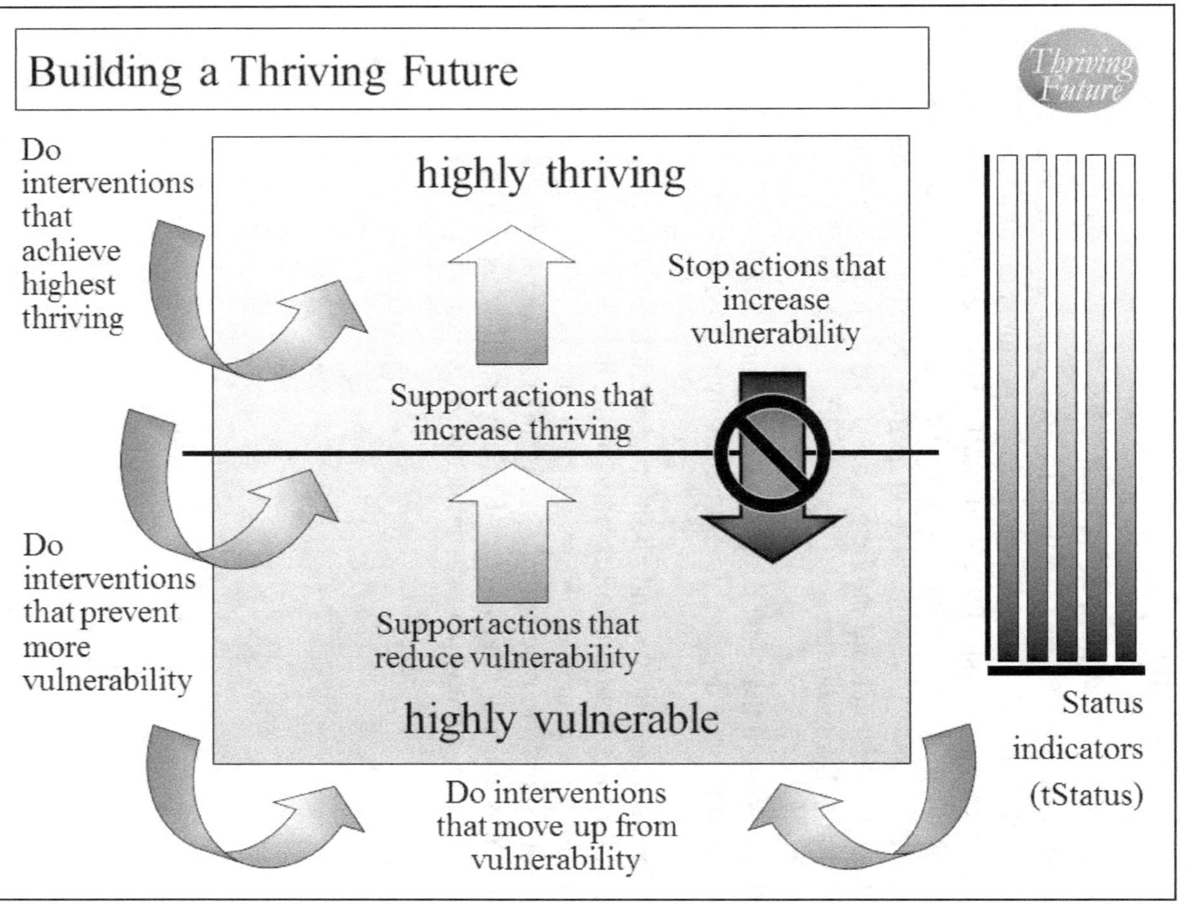

Figure 9.1. Building and Sustaining a Thriving Future.

With what result?

When successful, all of us, current and future, should be performing well. Be well-off (financially). Be well nourished (food and drink). Be well housed. Be well protected (exposures, crime). Be well educated. Be physically and mentally well (people). Personally grow/develop well. Be physically well (Earth, plants, animals, environment). Live within good habitat. Not be vulnerable. Produce personal and public goods. Live within a stable, positive climate. Be sustained.

But it is more than just people surviving and thriving. The Earth upon which we depend should be surviving and thriving.

When successful, we and all future generations achieve the surviving and thriving future for all forever, to the maximum extent possible. At this time in human history when we desire to thrive, when we need to survive, when our future is most endangered, and when we are most capable, the *Thrive!* **Endeavor**, all of us together, can and must build, achieve and sustain a thriving future for all forever.

Example and Worksheets

Example and Worksheets
for
You and Your Family and Friends

***Thrive!* Strategy and Action Plan** (Example of surviving and somewhat thriving).

Thriving and Surviving	How well (surviving/thriving) should your people as a whole be in near/long term future?	External/internal changes needed to achieve surviving and thriving future	Actions by your people and others Who will do what to/with whom, where, when, and with what result?
Performing (live/work/play) well?	*Jane has better job with better income, more certainty, pension, health benefits and no occupational exposure. John likes being electrician and continues but with more construction work.*	**External**: *Jane needs employer (current or a new one) to give her job with better income, more certainty, pension, health benefits and no occupational exposure. John needs home and business owners to do more construction and repair.*	**External by others**: *Community has begun seeking new employers with the intent of having 1000 new jobs within 12 months.* **Internal by your people**: *Jane will talk to current employer about higher pay and change in job to avoid exposure. John will approach home and business owners to get more jobs.*
		Internal:	**Internal by your people**: *Jane will more actively seek new job starting next Monday and, if feasible, change jobs to one with better income, more certainty, pension, health benefits and no occupational exposure within 3 months. John likes being electrician and continues but will market himself more and travel more within next two weeks.*
Well-off?	*Jane and John's employers provide better income security.*	**External**: *Need employers to provide better income security.*	**External by others**: *See above* **Internal by your people**: *See above*
		Internal:	**Internal by your people**: *See above*
Well nourished?	*Family has enough food but needs healthier diet, including reduced salt and saturated fat.*	**External**: *Need no-cost nutritionist/ dietician to help buying/preparing healthier diet, including reduced*	**External by others**: *Local grocery agrees to add more healthy food, on trial basis, within 30 days.*

		salt and saturated fat. situation. Need accessible and affordable healthy food source.	**Internal by your people:**
		Internal:	**Internal by your people:** *Family will shop for and help prepare healthier diet, including reduced salt and saturated fat, starting next Saturday. Family will avoid eating out in less healthy restaurants from today forward.*
Well housed	*Family improves home energy efficiency.*	**External:** *Need financial incentives to improve home energy efficiency, especially for heating during cold, harsh winters.*	**External by others:** *State may provide new energy efficiency incentives within 12 months but needs substantial public pressure within next 2 months.*
			Internal by your people:
		Internal:	**Internal by your people:** *Family will work to improve home energy efficiency doing as much as they can themselves and starting immediately.*
Well protected?	*Low crime is in work and home area.*	**External:** *Need police to continue to keep crime low in work and home area.*	**External by others:** *Low crime in work and home area may be enough. Community commits to sufficient funding to sustain effective police protection from this time forward.*
			Internal by your people:
		Internal:	**Internal by your people:** *Family will avoid situations where crime is more likely starting next weekend.*

Well educated?	*Jane and John have improved job skills for new and future jobs.*	**External**: *Need physically and financially accessible training program to improve job skills for new and future jobs.*	**External by others**: *Nearby community college will add re-training programs starting this fall session.*
			Internal by your people:
		Internal:	**Internal by your people**: *Jane and John will go through re-training to improve job skills for new and future jobs within next 6 months.*
Physically/ mentally well?	*Family improves mental health; Jane and John's job improvement helps. Family has improved physical and mental health by eating better, lowering stress, changing jobs, getting health benefits, and seeking better health care for more complex health problems.*	**External**: *Need physically and financially accessible mental health and physical health services that can successfully treat fairly complex problems.*	**External by others**: *Local health provider will add more mental health services within 12 months. More public health insurance programs are available that include physical and mental health services within 6 months.*
			Internal by your people:
		Internal:	**Internal by your people**: *Family will assist and support each other to improve mental health starting immediately. Job change and improvement will help (see above). Family will work together to improve physical and mental health by eating better, lowering stress, changing or improving jobs, getting health benefits, and seeking better health care from better providers for more complex health problems starting immediately.*
Growing/ developing	*Family has improved personal growth and*	**External**: *Need physically and*	**External by others**:

well?	*development at least in job/career.*	*financially accessible re-training programs.*	**Internal by your people:**
		Internal:	**Internal by your people:** *Family will improve personal growth and development, at least in job/career and re-training (see above)*
Living in good habitat?	*Habitat is beautiful and good.*	**External:** *No change needed, except to sustain habitat.*	**External by others:**
			Internal by your people: *Family will do volunteer work on protecting environment.*
		Internal:	**Internal by your people:** *Family will enjoy the beautiful and good habitat starting next weekend.*
Not vulnerable?	*Family minimizes vulnerability to job loss, health problems, low retirement resources. Children's school situation is good.*	**External:** *Need school and counselors to work successfully with Jane, John, Jim and Joan on improving children's school*	**External by others:**
			Internal by your people:
		Internal:	**Internal by your people:** *Jane and John will improve income security (see above). Family will work with school and counselors and with children to improve children's school situation starting with new school year.*
Producing personal/ public goods?	*Family produces thriving family life and high quality work products.*	**External:** *See above*	**External by others:** *School agrees to provide more support to children to produce better learning starting with new school year.*
			Internal by your people:

		Internal:	**Internal by your people**: *Family will join together to produce thriving family life (see above). Jane and John will produce high quality work products/services (see above).*
Stable, positive climate?	*Family is more energy efficient, especially for heating, to help with harsh, cold winters. Family takes positive advantage of climate. Family may move to more positive climate.*	**External**: *Need local heating fuel supplier to provide lower price heating fuel.*	**External by others**: *Local heating fuel supplier provides lower price heating fuel to avoid more competition effective immediately.*
			Internal by your people:
		Internal:	**Internal by your people**: *Family will be more energy efficient, especially for heating, which will help with harsh, cold winters starting this winter. Family will take better advantage of climate starting immediately. If they don't, they will explore moving to more positive climate within 2 years.*
Sustainable?	*Family ensures sustainability by working though marital issues, working through children's school issues, minimizing family stressors, improve retirement and savings, and improve health.*	**External**: *Need community, state and Federal social safety programs to receive stronger support and provide more assurance to family within 6 months. Need school and counselors to work successfully with Jane, John, Jim and Joan on improving children's school situation.*	**External by others**: *Community, state and Federal social safety programs receive stronger support and can provide more assurance to family within 6 months.*
			Internal by your people:

		Internal:	**Internal by your people**: *Family will ensure sustainability by getting better job situation, working though marital issues, working through children's school issues, minimizing family stressors, improve retirement and savings, and improve health within 12 months.*

Table 4.3b. How well should your future people as a whole be in near/long term future? What external/internal changes are needed to achieve your people's thriving future? To make this happen, what external/internal actions are needed?

Thrive!

Current and Future Persons (name)	For each person, have the person independently do a one-paragraph description in her/his own words. If the person can't, do one for the person. Cover things like work/living/playing, financial situation, eating/drinking, housing, protection, education, physical/mental health, growth/development, habitat, producing what, and climate. Enter the descriptions into this worksheet/table. Do a summary of your people as a whole.
Your current and future people as a whole. [Summary]	

Table 4.1. Who are your current and future people?

Thrive!

Current/Future Person: _____________________________ (Do for each person)

Thriving and Surviving	How well (surviving/ thriving) is the person?	What positively/ negatively impacts her/his thriving/ surviving?	[Optional] If no change, what is her/his near/ long term future behavior as to thriving/ surviving?
Performing (live/work/play) well?			
Well-off?			
Well nourished?			
Well housed?			
Well protected?			
Well educated?			
Physically/ mentally well?			
Growing/ developing well?			
Living in good habitat?			
Not vulnerable?			
Producing personal/ public goods?			
Stable, positive climate?			
Sustainable?			

Table 4.2a. How well (surviving/thriving) is the person? What positively/negatively impacts the person? What is her/his near/long term future behavior?

Thriving and Surviving	How well (surviving/ thriving) are your people as a whole?	What positively/ negatively impacts their thriving/ surviving?	[Optional] What is their near/ long term future behavior as to thriving/ surviving?
Performing (live/work/play) well?			
Well-off?			
Well nourished?			
Well housed?			
Well protected?			
Well educated?			
Physically/ mentally well?			
Growing/ developing well?			
Living in good habitat?			
Not vulnerable?			
Producing personal/ public goods?			
Stable, positive climate?			
Sustainable?			

Table 4.2b. How well (surviving/thriving) are your people as a whole? What positively/negatively impacts them? If no change, what is their near/long term future behavior?

Thriving and Surviving	How well (surviving/thriving) should your people as a whole be in near/long term future?	External/internal changes needed to achieve thriving/surviving future	External actions by others - Who externally will do what to/with whom, where, when, and with what result? How to make that happen?	Internal actions by your people - Who of your people will do what to/with whom, where, when, and with what result
Performing (live/work/play) well?				
Well-off?				
Well nourished?				
Well housed?				
Well protected?				
Well educated?				
Physically/mentally well?				
Growing/developing well?				
Living in good habitat?				
Not vulnerable?				
Producing personal/public goods?				
Stable, positive climate?				
Sustainable?				

Table 4.3a. *Thrive!* **Strategy and Action Plan.** How well (surviving/thriving) should your people as a whole be in near/long term future? What external/internal changes are needed to achieve your people's thriving future? To make this happen, what external/internal actions are needed?

Thrive!

Thriving and Surviving	How well (surviving/ thriving) should your people as a whole be in near/long term future?	External/internal changes needed to achieve surviving and thriving future	Actions by your people and others Who will do what to/with whom, where, when, and with what result?
Performing (live/work/ play) well?		External:	External by others:
			Internal by your people:
		Internal:	Internal by your people:
Well-off?		External:	External by others:
			Internal by your people:
		Internal:	Internal by your people:
Well nourished?		External:	External by others:
			Internal by your people:
		Internal:	Internal by your people:
Well housed		External:	External by others:
			Internal by your people:
		Internal:	Internal by your people:
Well protected?		External:	External by others:
			Internal by your people:
		Internal:	Internal by your people:
Well educated?		External:	External by others:
			Internal by your people:
		Internal:	Internal by your people:

Physically/ mentally well?		**External:**	**External by others:**
			Internal by your people:
		Internal:	**Internal by your people:**
Growing/ developing well?		**External:**	**External by others:**
			Internal by your people:
		Internal:	**Internal by your people:**
Living in good habitat?		**External:**	**External by others:**
			Internal by your people:
		Internal:	**Internal by your people:**
Not vulnerable?		**External:**	**External by others:**
			Internal by your people:
		Internal:	**Internal by your people:**
Producing personal/ public goods?		**External:**	**External by others:**
			Internal by your people:
		Internal:	**Internal by your people:**
Stable, positive climate?		**External:**	**External by others:**
			Internal by your people:
		Internal:	**Internal by your people:**
Sustainable?		**External:**	**External by others:**
			Internal by your people:
		Internal:	**Internal by your people:**

Table 4.3b. ***Thrive!*** **Strategy and Action Plan.** How well should your future people as a whole be in near/long term future? What external/internal changes are needed to achieve your people's thriving future? To make this happen, what external/internal actions are needed?

Example and Worksheets
for
You and Your Community

Thrive!

***Thrive!* Strategy and Action Plan** (Example of surviving and somewhat thriving).

Thriving and Surviving	How well (surviving/ thriving) should your community be in near/long term future?	External/internal changes needed to achieve surviving and thriving future	Actions by your community and others - Who will do what to/with whom, where, when, and with what result?
Performing (live/work/ play) well?	*Community should perform well with close to country's average mix lifestyles for city of its size. Unemployment should be 2 percentage points lower than country; mix of work should be similar to that of country as a whole and continue with a slightly larger percentage of blue collar workers and light industry.*	**External**: *Externally, outside employers should locate new jobs in community.*	**External by others**: *Outside employers locate new jobs in community within 12 months.*
			Internal by your community:
		Internal: *Internally, community should perform better than it has. Internally, community needs to gain more employers to get to 2 percentage points lower than country; community needs to gain more blue collar workers and light industry; internally, community employers should expand and add jobs.*	**Internal by your community**: *Community provides property tax incentives and community support within 12 months to gain more employers to get to 2 percentage points lower than country and to gain more blue collar workers and light industry; community employers expand and add 10% more jobs within 1 year. Community recruits outside 5 new employers to locate new jobs in community within 2 years.*
Well-off?	*Financial condition of community should be generally stable and sufficient to support public services; community should have slightly higher percentage of blue collar workers but who are no longer facing potential outsourcing of jobs and declining*	**External**: *Externally, outside employers should locate new jobs in community. .*	**External by others**: *Outside employers locate new jobs in community within 12 months.*
			Internal by your community: *Community provides incentives to outside employers to locate new jobs in community (see above).*

		Internal: *Internally, financial condition of community should be even better managed to be generally stable and sufficient to support public services; community should gain slightly higher percentage of blue collar workers; employers should avoid outsourcing of jobs and reducing union effectiveness*	**Internal by your community**: *Community better manages financial condition to be generally stable and sufficient to support public services starting next fiscal year; community retains and recruits employers to gain slightly higher percentage of blue collar workers (see above); employers avoid outsourcing of jobs and reducing union effectiveness over next 2 years.*
Well nourished?	*Food and drink should be available and affordable with prices 5% below average for country; community should have sufficient sources of healthy food; low income people should have adequate resources for healthy food and for food generally; community should have sufficient resources to feed very poor.*	**External**: *Externally, retail and wholesale food sources should hold down prices and add more healthy foods; country and state should provide resources to ensure food affordability for low and lower middle income persons.*	**External by others**: *Retail and wholesale food sources hold down prices to 1% increase for next 12 months and add more healthy foods on trial basis starting within 6 months; country and state provide resources this fiscal year to ensure food affordability for low and lower middle income persons.*
			Internal by your community: *Starting immediately, community with other communities presses retail and wholesale food sources to hold down prices and add more healthy foods; starting immediately, community with other communities presses country and state to provide resources to ensure food affordability for low and lower middle income persons.*

		Internal: *Internally, community, grocers and restaurants should make food and drink available and affordable with prices 5% below average for country; community, grocers and restaurants should have sufficient sources of healthy food; community should ensure low income people have adequate resources for healthy food and for food generally; community should add resources to have sufficient resources to feed very poor.*	**Internal by your community**: *Within 12 months, community, grocers and restaurants make food and drink available and affordable with prices 5% below average for country; community, grocers and restaurants provide sufficient sources of healthy food within 12 months; community provides support to low income people to ensure adequate resources for healthy food and for food generally within 12 months; community adds resources to have sufficient resources to feed very poor within 12 months.*
Well housed	*Housing for upper and middle income people should be available and affordable; housing for low and lower middle income people should be affordable, available and adequate.*	**External**: *Externally country and state should provide resources to build affordable housing and resources for lower middle and low income people to rent or buy a house.*	**External by others**: *Country and state provide resources to build affordable housing and resources for lower middle and low income people to rent or buy a house.*
			Internal by your community: *Starting immediately, community presses country and state to provide resources to build affordable housing and resources for lower middle and low income people to rent or buy a house.*

		Internal: *Internally, community should make available housing for low and lower middle income people that is affordable, available and adequate.*	**Internal by your community**: *Within 2 years, community should make available housing for low and lower middle income people that is affordable, available and adequate.*
Well protected?	*Community police force should be in top 10% for country; some neighborhood watch groups should exist but without any significant problems.*	**External**: *Externally, country and state should provide resources to adequately supplement community police resources.*	**External by others**: *Country and state provide resources this fiscal year to adequately supplement community police resources.*
			Internal by your community: *Starting immediately, community presses country and state to provide resources to adequately supplement community police resources.*
		Internal: *Internally, community should provide resources and management to ensure police force should be in top 10% for country; neighborhood watch groups should exercise good management to avoid any significant problems.*	**Internal by your community**: *Community provides resources and management this fiscal year to ensure police force is in top 10% for country; neighborhood watch groups exercise good management to avoid any significant problems starting within 30 days.*
Well educated?	*Education availability and quality should be in the top 10% of cities of its size; community should have slightly higher percentage of college educated.*	**External**: *Externally, country and state should provide resources to adequately supplement community education resources.*	**External by others**: *Country and state provide resources this fiscal year to adequately supplement community education resources.*
			Internal by your community: *Starting immediately, community presses country and state to provide resources to adequately supplement community education resources.*

		Internal: *Internally, community should provide resources and management to ensure education availability and quality in the top 10% of cities of its size; community should work to retain and increase the percentage of college educated.*	**Internal by your community**: *Community provides resources and management this fiscal year to ensure education availability and quality in the top 10% of cities of its size; starting immediately, community works to retain and increase the percentage of college educated.*
Physically/ mentally well?	*Physical and mental health should be in top 10% of cities of its size; community should have substantially less occupationally related illness; private health services should be in top 25% and public health services should be in top 25% of cities of its size.*	**External**: *Externally, country and state should ensure affordability (cost and insurance) of health services.*	**External by others**: *Country and state ensure affordability (cost and insurance) of health services by instituting cost constraints to less than 3% increase and providing affordable health insurance within 12 months.*
			Internal by your community: *Starting immediately, community presses country and state to ensure affordability (cost and insurance) of health services.*

		Internal: *Internally, community and private and public health services should improve services so that physical and mental health should be in top 10% of cities of its size; community and industry should ensure having substantially less occupationally related illness; community and private health services should ensure private health services in top 25% and community should ensure public health services in top 25% of cities of its size.*	**Internal by your community**: *Within 2 years, community and private and public health services improve services so that physical and mental health should be in top 10% of cities of its size; community and industry ensure having substantially less occupationally related illness within 2 years; community and private health services ensure private health services in top 25% within 2 years; community manages and provides resources this fiscal year to ensure public health services in top 25% of cities of its size.*
Growing/ developing well?	*Personal growth and development should be substantially better than cities of its size and community should have job re-training in top 10% of its size.*	**External**: *Externally, country and state should provide additional re-training resources to supplement community.*	**External by others**: *Country and state provide additional re-training resources this fiscal year to supplement community.*
			Internal by your community: *Starting immediately, community presses country and state to provide additional re-training resources to supplement community.*

		Internal: *Internally, community should help ensure personal growth and development is substantially better than cities of its size; community should ensure job re-training is in top 10% of its size.*	**Internal by your community**: *Community helps ensure personal growth and development is substantially better than cities of its size within 18 months; community adds resources this fiscal year to ensure job re-training is in top 10% of its size.*
Living in good habitat?	*Habitat should be very pleasant and very healthy.*	**External**: *Externally, country and state should ensure habitat is very pleasant and very healthy.*	**External by others**: *Country and state ensure habitat is very pleasant and very healthy by adding 25% more funding this fiscal year for public parks and preventive health programs.*
			Internal by your community: *Starting immediately, community presses country and state to ensure habitat is very pleasant and very healthy.*
		Internal: *Internally, community should ensure habitat is very pleasant and very healthy.*	**Internal by your community**: *Within 1 year, community implements policies to ensure habitat is very pleasant and very healthy.*

Not vulnerable?	*Community should have much less vulnerability; community should greatly reduce its vulnerability on job and income loss, affordable and healthy foods, affordable housing, public health services, and community revenues.*	**External**: *Externally, country and state should reduce vulnerability country and state-wide with special efforts (as listed for other areas) to greatly reduce its vulnerability on job and income loss, affordable and healthy foods, affordable housing, public health services, and community revenues.*	**External by others**: *Within 2 years, country and state policies and programs substantially reduce vulnerability country and state-wide with special efforts (as listed for other areas) to greatly reduce its vulnerability on job and income loss, affordable and healthy foods, affordable housing, public health services, and community revenues.*
			Internal by your community: *Starting immediately, community presses country and state to institute policies and programs that reduce vulnerability country and state-wide with special efforts (as listed for other areas) to greatly reduce its vulnerability on job and income loss, affordable and healthy foods, affordable housing, public health services, and community revenues.*
		Internal: *Internally, community should reduce its vulnerabilities with special efforts (as listed for other areas) to greatly reduce its vulnerability on job and income loss, affordable and healthy foods, affordable housing, public health services, and community revenues.*	**Internal by your community**: *Within 2 years, community substantially reduces its vulnerabilities with special efforts (as listed for other areas) to greatly reduce its vulnerability on job and income loss, affordable and healthy foods, affordable housing, public health services, and community revenues.*

Producing personal/ public goods?	*Community should produce a wider range of products and services for city of its size, a substantially higher percentage of higher quality manufactured products, a high percentage of healthy and well educated children and a range of recreational activities in the top 10% of cities of its size.*	**External**: *Externally, employers should bring more and a wider range of jobs and higher quality manufacturing; country and state provide added education resources; country and state add recreational resources to community.*	**External by others**: *Employers bring more and a wider range of jobs and higher quality manufacturing within 12 months; country and state provide added education resources this fiscal year; country and state add recreational resources this fiscal year to community.*
			Internal by your community: *Community recruits employers to bring more and a wider range of jobs and higher quality manufacturing within 12 months; starting immediately, community presses country and state to provide added education resources; starting immediately, community presses country and state to add recreational resources to community.*

		Internal: *Internally, community should ensure a wider range of products and services than other cities of its size, a substantially higher percentage of higher quality manufactured products, a high percentage of healthy and well educated children and a range of recreational activities in the top 10% of cities of its size.*	Internal by your community: *Community and private sector ensure a wider range of products and services than other cities of its size and a substantially higher percentage of higher quality manufactured products within 12 months; community ensures supportive resources this fiscal year to help ensure a high percentage of healthy and well educated children; and community provides resources this fiscal year to ensure a range of recreational activities in the top 10% of cities of its size.*
Stable, positive climate?	*Climate should continue to be good to very good.*	External: *Externally, country and state work to ensure climate is good to very good.*	External by others: *Country and state work to ensure climate is good to very good through environmental policy within 18 months and international agreements within 2 years.*
			Internal by your community:
		Internal:	Internal by your community:
Sustainable?	*Sustainability should be ensured and no longer be in question in spite of changing national and international economics and potential job outsourcing.*	External: *Externally, country and state support policies that reduce outsourcing and protect jobs in community.*	External by others: *Country and state execute policies that reduce outsourcing and protect jobs in community within 12 months.*

			Internal by your community: *Starting immediately, community presses country and state to support policies that reduce outsourcing and protect jobs in community*
		Internal: *Internally, community ensures sustainability is no longer in question in spite of changing national and international economics and potential job outsourcing.*	**Internal by your community**: *Starting immediately, community presses country and state to ensure climate is good to very good. Within 2 years, community ensures sustainability is no longer in question in spite of changing national and international economics and potential job outsourcing.*

Table 5.4. *Thrive!* **Strategy and Action Plan.** How well (surviving/thriving) should your community be in near/long term future? What external/internal changes are needed to achieve your community's thriving future? To make this happen, what external/internal actions are needed?

Community Characteristics	What is your community today?
Geographic boundaries	
Gender make-up	
Age make-up	
Racial make-up	
Ethnic make-up	
Lifestyle	
Type of work	
Financial situation	
Food/drink	
Housing	
Protection	
Education	
Physical / mental health	
Personal growth / development	
Habitat	
Producing what	
Climate	
Sustainability	

Table 5.1. What is your community today?

Thriving and Surviving	How well (surviving/ thriving) is your community?	What positively/ negatively impacts its thriving/ surviving?	What is its near/ long term behavior as to thriving/ surviving?
Performing (live/work/play) well?			
Well-off?			
Well nourished?			
Well housed?			
Well protected?			
Well educated?			
Physically/ mentally well?			
Growing/ developing well?			
Living in good habitat?			
Not vulnerable?			
Producing personal/ public goods?			
Stable, positive climate?			
Sustainable?			

Table 5.2. How well (surviving/thriving) is your community? What positively/ negatively impacts it? If no change, what is its near/long term future behavior?

Community Characteristics	What is your desired and/or likely future community?
Type of work/how people live	
Financial situation	
Food/drink	
Housing	
Protection	
Education	
Physical / mental health	
Personal growth / development	
Habitat	
Producing what	
Climate	
Sustainability	

Table 5.3. What is your desired and/or likely future community?

Thriving and Surviving	How well (surviving/ thriving) should your community be in near/long term future?	External/internal changes needed to achieve surviving and thriving future	Actions by your community and others - Who will do what to/with whom, where, when, and with what result?
Performing (live/work/ play) well?		External:	External by others:
			Internal by your community:
		Internal:	Internal by your community:
Well-off?		External:	External by others:
			Internal by your community:
		Internal:	Internal by your community:
Well nourished?		External:	External by others:
			Internal by your community:
		Internal:	Internal by your community:
Well housed		External:	External by others:
			Internal by your community:
		Internal:	Internal by your community:
Well protected?		External:	External by others:
			Internal by your community:
		Internal:	Internal by your community:
Well educated?		External:	External by others:
			Internal by your community:
		Internal:	Internal by your community:
Physically/ mentally well?		External:	External by others:
			Internal by your community:
		Internal:	Internal by your community:

Growing/ developing well?		**External:**	**External by others:**
			Internal by your community:
		Internal:	**Internal by your community:**
Living in good habitat?		**External:**	**External by others:**
			Internal by your community:
		Internal:	**Internal by your community:**
Not vulnerable?		**External:**	**External by others:**
			Internal by your community:
		Internal:	**Internal by your community:**
Producing personal/ public goods?		**External:**	**External by others:**
			Internal by your community:
		Internal:	**Internal by your community:**
Stable, positive climate?		**External:**	**External by others:**
			Internal by your community:
		Internal:	**Internal by your community:**
Sustainable?		**External:**	**External by others:**
			Internal by your community:
		Internal:	**Internal by your community:**

Table 5.4. *Thrive!* **Strategy and Action Plan.** How well (surviving/thriving) should your community be in near/long term future? What external/internal changes are needed to achieve your community's thriving future? To make this happen, what external/internal actions are needed?

Example and Worksheets
for
You and Your Country

Thrive!

***Thrive!* Strategy and Action Plan** (Example of surviving and somewhat thriving).

Thriving and Surviving	How well (surviving/ thriving) should your country be in near/long term future?	External/internal changes needed to achieve surviving and thriving future	Actions by your country and others - Who will do what to/with whom, where, when, and with what result?
Performing (live/work/ play) well?	*Country should perform better than countries on its continent with close to continent's average mix of lifestyles for country of its size. Unemployment should be lower than its continent; mix of work should be similar to that of its continent but with a larger percentage of blue collar and of agricultural workers and light industry.*	**External**: *Externally, more business, agriculture and light industry should move into country with more employment for blue collar and agriculture workers.*	**External by others**: *Twenty-five percent more business, agriculture and light industry move into country with more employment for blue collar and agriculture workers within 2 years.* **Internal by your country**:
		Internal: *Internally, country should have a better, more collaborative government with a collaborative partnership with the private sector committed to perform better than countries on its continent. Internally, more business, agriculture and light industry should stay in country with more employment for blue collar and agriculture workers.*	**Internal by your country**: *Within 1 year, country builds and sustains a better, more collaborative government with a collaborative partnership with the private sector committed to perform better than countries on its continent. With small incentives added by government, 95% of business, agriculture and light industry stay in country with more employment for blue collar and agriculture workers. With small incentives added by government, 25 percent more business, agriculture and light industry move into country within 2 years with more employment for blue collar and agriculture workers.*
Well-off?	*Financial condition of country should*	**External**:	**External by others**: **Internal by your country**:

	blue collar workers who should not face potential moving of jobs out of country.	**Internal**: *Internally, government and private sector should collaborate and ensure financial condition is stable and sufficient to support needed public services; employers should be committed to blue collar workers and not moving their jobs out of country; country and employers should have expanded job training.*	**Internal by your country**: *Government and private sector collaborate and come to agreement this year and ensure financial condition is stable and sufficient to support needed public services for at least next 5 years; employers commit to blue collar workers and not moving their jobs out of country for at least next 5 years; country and employers expand job training by 50% within 1 year with 50/50 funding.*
Well nourished?	*Food and drink should be available and prices should be 10% below average for its continent; country should have sufficient sources of healthy food; low income people should have resources for healthy food and for food generally; country should have sufficient resources to feed very poor.*	**External**:	**External by others**:
			Internal by your country:
		Internal: *Internally, food and drink producers, wholesalers and retailers should ensure food and drink is available and 10% below average cost for its continent; country and food industry should ensure sufficient sources of healthy food; country should ensure low income people have resources for healthy food and for food generally; country should ensure sufficient resources to feed very poor.*	**Internal by your country**: *Food and drink producers, wholesalers and retailers ensure food and drink is available and 10% below average cost for its continent for at least next 3 years; country and food industry agree to and ensure sufficient sources of healthy food for at least next 3 years; country comes to agreement, provides funding and helps ensure low income people have resources for healthy food and for food generally for at least next 5 years; country comes to agreement, provides funding and ensures sufficient resources to feed very poor for at least next 5 years.*
Well housed	*Housing for upper and middle income*	**External**:	**External by others**:
			Internal by your country:

	and lower middle income people should be available, affordable and adequate.	**Internal**: *Internally, banks and housing industry should ensure housing for upper and middle income people is available and affordable; government, bankers and builders should ensure housing for low and lower middle income people is available, affordable and adequate.*	**Internal by your country**: *Banks and housing industry continue to ensure housing for upper and middle income people is available and affordable for at least next 5 years; government, bankers and builders come to agreement, government provides incentive funding and all ensure housing for low and lower middle income people is available, affordable and adequate within 5 years.*
Well protected?	*Country local police force, state police force and country military should be best for its continent.*	**External**:	**External by others**:
			Internal by your country:
		Internal: *Internally, country and its local police force, state police force and country military should ensure it is best of its continent, including adequate resourcing.*	**Internal by your country**: *Country and its local police force, state police force and country military ensure it is best of its continent, including strong management and adequate resourcing for at least next 5 years.*
Well educated?	*Education availability and quality should be best on its continent; country should have 10 percent more college educated than its continent.*	**External**:	**External by others**:
			Internal by your country:
		Internal: *Internally, country and its education people should ensure education availability and quality is best on its continent and should ensure country has 10 percent more college educated than its continent.*	**Internal by your country**: *Country and its education people come to agreement within 1 year; government provides funding; and all ensure education availability and quality is best on its continent and ensure country has 10 percent more college educated than its continent for at least next 5 years.*
Physically/ mentally well?	*Physical and mental health should be best*	**External**:	**External by others**:
			Internal by your country:

	substantially less occupationally related illness; private and public health services should be best on its continent.	**Internal**: *Internally, country and its private and public health services should ensure physical and mental health is best compared to other countries on its continent; country and employers should ensure workers have substantially less occupationally related illness; country and private and public health services should ensure services are best on its continent; country should ensure every person without private insurance has financial access to needed health services; country and its people should ensure each person is improving personal and family health.*	**Internal by your country**: *Country and its private and public health services agree and within 2 years ensure physical and mental health is best compared to other countries on its continent; country and employers agree within 1 year and ensure workers have substantially less occupationally related illness; country and private and public health services agree within 1 year and ensure services are best on its continent within 2 years; country agrees within 1 year, provides funding for at least 5 years, and ensures every person without private insurance has financial access to needed health services for at least the next 5 years; country and its people begin collaborative effort this year and ensure each person is improving personal and family health starting within 2 years.*
Growing/ developing well?	*Personal growth and development should be better than countries on its continent and have substantially more job training.*	**External**:	**External by others**:
			Internal by your country:
		Internal: *Internally, country and its people should ensure personal growth and development is better than countries on its continent; country and employers should ensure substantially more job training.*	**Internal by your country**: *Country and its people begin collaborative effort this year and ensure personal growth and development is better than countries on its continent within 2 years; country and employers agree within 1 year and agree to 50/50 funding ensure substantially more job training within 1 year.*

Living in good habitat?	*Habitat should have the best mix of pleasant and harsh and healthy and unhealthy on its continent.*	**External**: *Externally, country and its neighboring countries should jointly ensure habitat has the best mix of pleasant and harsh and healthy and unhealthy.*	**External by others**: *Neighboring countries agree within 1 year and jointly help ensure habitat has the best mix of pleasant and harsh and healthy and unhealthy with phased plan over next 5 years.*
			Internal by your country: *Starting immediately, country joins with neighboring countries, agree within 1 year, and jointly help ensure habitat has the best mix of pleasant and harsh and healthy and unhealthy with phased plan over next 5 years.*
		Internal: *Internally, country and its people should ensure habitat has the best mix of pleasant and harsh and healthy and unhealthy on its continent.*	**Internal by your country**: *Country and its people develop collaborative effort and strategy and, within 5 years, ensure habitat has the best mix of pleasant and harsh and healthy and unhealthy on its continent.*
Not vulnerable?	*While country has had much vulnerability, it should no longer be vulnerable on job loss, limited income, lack of affordable and healthy foods, lack of affordable and adequate housing for poorer people, inadequate private and public health services, and low country revenues.*	**External**:	**External by others**:
			Internal by your country:
		Internal: *Internally, while country has had much vulnerability, country and its people should ensure it is no longer vulnerable on job loss, limited income, lack of affordable and healthy foods, lack of affordable and adequate housing for poorer people, inadequate private and public health services, and low country revenues.*	**Internal by your country**: *While country has had much vulnerability, country and its people collaborate, develop strategy and, within 1 year start to ensure it is no longer vulnerable on job loss, limited income, lack of affordable and healthy foods, lack of affordable and adequate housing for poorer people, inadequate private and public health services, and low country revenues.*
Producing personal/ public	*Compared to its continent, country should*	**External**:	**External by others**:
			Internal by your country:

		Internal: *Internally and compared to its continent, country and its people should ensure it produces an optimal range of products and services for its continent, a substantially higher percentage of high quality manufactured products, the best percentage of healthy and well educated children and a wide range of recreational activities.*	Internal by your country: *Within 5 years and compared to its continent, country and its people work together to ensure it produces an optimal range of products and services for its continent, a substantially higher percentage of high quality manufactured products, the best percentage of healthy and well educated children on its continent and a wide range of recreational activities.*
	products and services for its continent, a substantially higher percentage of high quality manufactured products, the best percentage of healthy and well educated children and a wide range of recreational activities.		
Stable, positive climate?	*Climate should be very good and stay that way.*	External: *Externally, country should join with international community to ensure climate is very good and stays that way.*	External by others: *International community comes to agreement within 2 years and ensures climate is very good and stays that way for centuries to come.*
			Internal by your country: *Starting immediately, country joins with international community, comes to agreement within 2 years and ensures climate is very good and stays that way for centuries to come.*
		Internal:	Internal by your country:
Sustainable?	*Sustainability should be ensured and no longer be in question due to potential job losses, limited income and country revenues, lower education and health, under developed natural resources and changing national and international*	External: *Externally, country should join with neighboring countries and international community to ensure no negative impact from changing national and international economics.*	External by others: *Neighboring countries and international community come to agreement within 1 year and help ensure no negative impact from changing national and international economics for at least next 10 years.*
			Internal by your country: *Starting immediately, country joins with neighboring countries and international community, comes to agreement within 1 year and helps ensure no negative impact from changing national and international economics for at least the next 10 years.*

	economics.	**Internal**: *Internally, country and its people should ensure sustainability and that there is no longer job losses, limited income and country revenues, lower education and health, under developed natural resources and no negative impact from changing national and international economics.*	**Internal by your country**: *Country and its people collaborate, develop strategy and, within 1 year work to ensure sustainability and that there is no longer job losses, limited income and country revenues, lower education and health, under developed natural resources and negative impact from changing national and international economics for at least next 10 years.*

Table 6.4. *Thrive!* **Strategy and Action Plan.** How well (surviving/thriving) should your country be in near/long term future? What external/internal changes are needed to achieve your country's thriving future? To make this happen, what external/internal actions are needed?

Country Characteristics	What is your country today?
Geographic boundaries	
Gender make-up	
Age make-up	
Racial make-up	
Ethnic make-up	
Lifestyle	
Type of work	
Financial situation	
Food/drink	
Housing	
Protection	
Education	
Physical / mental health	
Personal growth / development	
Habitat	
Producing what	
Climate	
Sustainability	

Table 6.1. What is your country today?

Thriving and Surviving	How well (surviving/ thriving) is your country?	What positively/ negatively impacts its thriving/ surviving?	What is its near/ long term behavior as to thriving/ surviving?
Performing (live/work/play) well?			
Well-off?			
Well nourished?			
Well housed?			
Well protected?			
Well educated?			
Physically/ mentally well?			
Growing/ developing well?			
Living in good habitat?			
Not vulnerable?			
Producing personal/ public goods?			
Stable, positive climate?			
Sustainable?			

Table 6.2. How well (surviving/thriving) is your country? What positively/ negatively impacts it? What is its near/long term future behavior?

Country Characteristics	What is your desired and/or likely future country?
Type of work/how people live	
Financial situation	
Food/drink	
Housing	
Protection	
Education	
Physical / mental health	
Personal growth / development	
Habitat	
Producing what	
Climate	
Sustainability	

Table 6.3. What is your desired and/or likely future country?

Thriving and Surviving	How well (surviving/ thriving) should your country be in near/long term future?	External/internal changes needed to achieve surviving and thriving future	Actions by your country and others - Who will do what to/with whom, where, when, and with what result?
Performing (live/work/ play) well?		External:	External by others:
			Internal by your country:
		Internal:	Internal by your country:
Well-off?		External:	External by others:
			Internal by your country:
		Internal:	Internal by your country:
Well nourished?		External:	External by others:
			Internal by your country:
		Internal:	Internal by your country:
Well housed		External:	External by others:
			Internal by your country:
		Internal:	Internal by your country:
Well protected?		External:	External by others:
			Internal by your country:
		Internal:	Internal by your country:
Well educated?		External:	External by others:
			Internal by your country:
		Internal:	Internal by your country:
Physically/ mentally well?		External:	External by others:
			Internal by your country:
		Internal:	Internal by your country:

Growing/ developing well?		External:	External by others:
			Internal by your country:
		Internal:	Internal by your country:
Living in good habitat?		External:	External by others:
			Internal by your country:
		Internal:	Internal by your country:
Not vulnerable?		External:	External by others:
			Internal by your country:
		Internal:	Internal by your country:
Producing personal/ public goods?		External:	External by others:
			Internal by your country:
		Internal:	Internal by your country:
Stable, positive climate?		External:	External by others:
			Internal by your country:
		Internal:	Internal by your country:
Sustainable?		External:	External by others:
			Internal by your country:
		Internal:	Internal by your country:

Table 6.4. *Thrive!* **Strategy and Action Plan.** How well (surviving/thriving) should your country be in near/long term future? What external/internal changes are needed to achieve your country's thriving future? To make this happen, what external/internal actions are needed?

Example and Worksheets
for
Our World

Thrive!

Thrive! **Strategy and Action Plan** (Example of surviving and thriving).

Thriving and Surviving	How well (surviving/ thriving) should our world be in near/long term future?	Changes needed to achieve surviving and thriving future	Actions - Who will do what to/with whom, where, when, and with what result?
			Starting immediately, we (people, business/industry, private organizations (local, country), governments (local, country) and international organizations) build, achieve, and sustain a surviving and thriving future for our world and for all forever, including:
Performing (live/work/ play) well?	Our world and our people should be performing (living, working, recreating, learning) well enough to survive and thrive. *For example. All live, work, recreate and learn well.*	*People, business/industry, private organizations (local, country), governments (local, country) and international organizations act to ensure a) all (who are able and not appropriately retired) can work and earn a living income sufficient to survive and thrive and b) all have sufficient resources for and are living, recreating, learning so that they are surviving and thriving to maximum extent feasible.*	*Starting immediately, people, business/industry, private organizations (local, country), governments (local, country) and international organizations act to ensure, within the next 20 years, a) all (who are able and not appropriately retired) can work and earn a living income sufficient to survive and thrive and b) all have sufficient resources for and are living, recreating, learning so that they are surviving and thriving to maximum extent feasible.*
Well-off?	Our world and our people should be well-off (financially) enough to survive and thrive. *For example. A living income for all, eliminate poverty.*	*People, business/industry, private organizations (local, country), governments (local, country) and international organizations act to ensure a) all have sufficient income/resources to survive and thrive and b) all governments have sufficient resources to*	*Starting immediately, people, business/industry, private organizations (local, country), governments (local, country) and international organizations act to ensure, within the next 20 years, a) all have sufficient income/resources to survive and thrive and b) all governments have*

		provide needed (supporting surviving) and desired (supporting thriving) public programs and policies.	*sufficient resources to provide needed (supporting surviving) and desired (supporting thriving) public programs and policies.*
Well nourished?	Our world and our people should be well nourished (food and drink) enough to survive and thrive. *For example, Affordable and healthy food for all.*	*People, business/industry, private organizations (local, country), governments (local, country) and international organizations act to ensure that all people have access to, be able to afford and consume healthy foods enough to survive and thrive.*	*Starting immediately, people, business/industry, private organizations (local, country), governments (local, country) and international organizations act to ensure, within the next 20 years, that all people have access to, be able to afford and consume healthy foods enough to survive and thrive.*
Well housed?	Our world and our people should be well housed enough to survive and thrive. *For example. Affordable and adequate housing for all.*	*People, business/industry, private organizations (local, country), governments (local, country) and international organizations act to ensure all have access to, be able to afford and live in adequate and preferably high performing housing that supports surviving and thriving.*	*Starting immediately, people, business/industry, private organizations (local, country), governments (local, country) and international organizations act to ensure, within the next 20 years, all have access to, be able to afford and live in adequate and preferably high performing housing that supports surviving and thriving.*
Well protected?	Our world and our people should be well protected (exposures, crime) enough to survive and thrive. *For example. All are protected from crime and environmental threats.*	*People, business/industry, private organizations (local, country), governments (local, country) and international organizations act to ensure a) environmental exposures in home, workplace and elsewhere are minimized so as to not prevent surviving and thriving and b) crimes are minimized in terms of frequency and impact so as to not prevent surviving and thriving.*	*Starting immediately, people, business/industry, private organizations (local, country), governments (local, country) and international organizations act to ensure, within the next 20 years, a) environmental exposures in home, workplace and elsewhere are minimized so as to not prevent surviving and thriving and b) crimes are minimized to the extent feasible in terms of frequency and impact so as to not prevent surviving*

			and thriving.
Well educated?	Our world and our people should be well educated enough to survive and thrive. *For example. All are well educated with all reaching optimum educational levels.*	*People, business/industry, private organizations (local, country), governments (local, country) and international organizations act to ensure all people are educated to the full extent of their abilities, needs and desires and to support their surviving and thriving.*	*Starting immediately, people, business/industry, private organizations (local, country), governments (local, country) and international organizations act to ensure, within the next 20 years, all people are educated to the full extent of their abilities, needs and desires and to support their surviving and thriving.*
Physically/ mentally well?	Our world and our people should be physically and mentally well enough to survive and thrive. *For example. All are physically and mentally healthy.*	*People, business/industry, private organizations (local, country), governments (local, country) and international organizations act to ensure a) all people receive the optimal health support to ensure surviving and thriving and b) all people's physical and mental health is optimized to best ensure surviving and thriving.*	*Starting immediately, people, business/industry, private organizations (local, country), governments (local, country) and international organizations act to ensure, within the next 20 years, a) all people receive the optimal health support to ensure, within the next 20 years, surviving and thriving and b) all people's physical and mental health is optimized to best ensure surviving and thriving.*
Growing/ developing well?	Our world and our people should be personally growing/developing well enough to survive and thrive. *For example. All are growing and developing to their full potential.*	*People, business/industry, private organizations (local, country), governments (local, country) and international organizations act to ensure all people are personally growing and developing to best ensure surviving and thriving.*	*Starting immediately, people, business/industry, private organizations (local, country), governments (local, country) and international organizations act to ensure, within the next 20 years, all people are personally growing and developing to best ensure surviving and thriving.*
Living in good habitat?	Our world should be good habitat enough	*People, business/industry, private organizations (local, country),*	*Starting immediately, people, business/industry, private organizations*

	to survive and thrive. *For example. All live in good, sustainable habitat including housing, community, and natural environment.*	*governments (local, country) and international organizations act to ensure a) all people have access to habitat that best supports their surviving and thriving and b) our world has the optimal mix, quantity and quality of habitat to best support our world and its inhabitants' surviving and thriving.*	*(local, country), governments (local, country) and international organizations act to ensure, within the next 20 years, a) all people have access to habitat that best supports their surviving and thriving and b) our world has the optimal mix, quantity and quality of habitat to best support our world and its inhabitants' surviving and thriving.*
Not vulnerable?	Our world and our people should not be vulnerable. *For example. Vulnerability is minimized in terms of frequency, level, duration and impact.*	*People, business/industry, private organizations (local, country), governments (local, country) and international organizations act to ensure our world and all of its people, if vulnerable, are vulnerable only to the minimum extent feasible.*	*Starting immediately, people, business/industry, private organizations (local, country), governments (local, country) and international organizations act to ensure, within the next 20 years, our world and all of its people, if vulnerable, are vulnerable only to the minimum extent feasible.*
Producing personal/ public goods?	Our world and our people should be producing personal and public goods enough to survive and thrive. *For example. Should produce optimal personal income/resources, housing, food and drink, energy, education, health, protection, personal growth and development, and habitat.*	*People, business/industry, private organizations (local, country), governments (local, country) and international organizations act to ensure our people produce personal and public goods (including personal income/resources, housing, food and drink, energy, education, health, protection, personal growth and development, and habitat) so as to support surviving and thriving for all persons and for our world overall.*	*Starting immediately, people, business/industry, private organizations (local, country), governments (local, country) and international organizations act to ensure, within the next 20 years, our people produce personal and public goods (including personal income/resources, housing, food and drink, energy, education, health, protection, personal growth and development, and habitat) so as to support surviving and thriving for all persons and for our world overall.*

Stable, positive climate?	Our world should have a stable, positive climate. *For example. Our climate should help support all human, animal and plant life forever.*	*People, business/industry, private organizations (local, country), governments (local, country) and international organizations act to ensure all people behave so as to avoid negative impacts and support positive impacts so as to help ensure a stable, positive climate.*	*Starting immediately, people, business/industry, private organizations (local, country), governments (local, country) and international organizations act to ensure, within the next 10 years, all people behave so as to avoid negative impacts and support positive impacts so as to help ensure a stable, positive climate.*
Sustainable?	Our world and our people should be sustained. *For example. Our people and our earth are sustained for all forever.*	*People, business/industry, private organizations (local, country), governments (local, country) and international organizations act to ensure all people behave so as to ensure the sustainability of our world <u>and</u> its people.*	*Starting immediately, people, business/industry, private organizations (local, country), governments (local, country) and international organizations act to ensure, within the next 5 years, all people behave so as to ensure the sustainability of our world <u>and</u> its people.*

Table 7.4. ***Thrive!* Strategy and Action Plan.** How well (surviving/thriving) should our world be in near/long term future? What changes are needed to achieve our world's thriving future? To make this happen, what actions are needed?

World Characteristics	What is our world today?
Geographic boundaries	
Gender make-up	
Age make-up	
Racial make-up	
Ethnic make-up	
Lifestyle	
Type of work	
Financial situation	
Food/drink	
Housing	
Protection	
Education	
Physical / mental health	
Personal growth / development	
Habitat	
Producing what	
Climate	
Sustainability	

Table 7.1. What is our world today?

Thriving and Surviving	How well (surviving/ thriving) is our world?	What positively/ negatively impacts its thriving/ surviving?	What is its near/ long term behavior as to thriving/ surviving?
Performing (live/work/play) well?			
Well-off?			
Well nourished?			
Well housed?			
Well protected?			
Well educated?			
Physically/ mentally well?			
Growing/ developing well?			
Living in good habitat?			
Not vulnerable?			
Producing personal/ public goods?			
Stable, positive climate?			
Sustainable?			

Table 7.2. How well (surviving/thriving) is our world? What positively/ negatively impacts it? What is its near/long term future behavior?

World Characteristics	What is our desired and/or likely future world?
Type of work/how people live	
Financial situation	
Food/drink	
Housing	
Protection	
Education	
Physical / mental health	
Personal growth / development	
Habitat	
Producing what	
Climate	
Sustainability	

Table 7.3. What is our desired and/or likely future world?

Thriving and Surviving	How well (surviving/ thriving) should our world be in near/long term future?	Changes needed to achieve surviving and thriving future	Actions - Who will do what to/with whom, where, when, and with what result?
Performing (live/work/play) well?			
Well-off?			
Well nourished?			
Well housed?			
Well protected?			
Well educated?			
Physically/ mentally well?			
Growing/ developing well?			
Living in good habitat?			
Not vulnerable?			
Producing personal/ public goods?			
Stable, positive climate?			
Sustainable?			

Table 7.4. *Thrive!* **Strategy and Action Plan.** How well (surviving/thriving) should our world be in near/long term future? What changes are needed to achieve our world's thriving future? To make this happen, what actions are needed?